Red or Blue?

This Book is 4 U!

I0101838

Dedication

This book is dedicated to my wife and companion whom I love, and my three sons: Scott, the educator; John, the engineer; and Thomas, the artist.

Table of Contents

Preface

The two subjects most often debated and most often unchanged by debate are religion and politics. Our family enjoys a tradition of having Sunday brunch after church where we discuss daily issues and all too frequently the discussion drifts into politics.   These political discussions, like similar discussions with friends for the past two decades, have been mostly centered on the degradation of the American federal government. Every year the government grows, makes undeliverable promises and sinks further into debt with no real expectation that these trends will change. Every year the country grows more divided politically and the citizens are becoming even more polarized on issues. It is all too simple to blame the two political parties who argue constantly and denigrate each other personally and politically, but in the end do the same thing: expand an increasingly ineffective federal government.

Most of the time when the family discusses federal politics, the verbiage turns very negative due to the frustration induced by a presumed position that there is nothing a family can do that would actually change the dynamics of a failing federal government. One of our family principles is not to allow our Sunday discussions to become meaningless complaining sessions, but to follow debate with a discussion of ways to improve the situation.   Positive and feasible political recommendations have, until now, been all too elusive.

We feel that the failing government is not best described as between Democrats and Republicans or their campaigning issues and methods.   We do feel that the individual citizens have very strong beliefs and expectations of government duties and responsibilities. These feelings are deeply divided across this nation. We think that the best way to generalize this difference in common terms is that "red" states and "blue" states are just plain different in very basic and fundamental ways. It is also apparent that the philosophical differences between red and blue states are widening and increasingly exacerbated by uncompromising and nonproductive Washington politics.

I feel that the issue is not whether the blue state philosophy is right and the red state philosophy is wrong, or vice versa. Actually each of the different philosophies has adequate valid justifications for their actions. The great national division, in my opinion, is that on one hand the red state advocates demand that the blue state believers adopt red state philosophy and abandon blue state principles, and on the other hand the blue state advocates demand that the red state believers adopt blue state philosophy and abandon red state principles.

The objective of this book is to suggest a plan that would directly address the red state and blue state division wherein both sides would be able follow their dreams without the interference of the opposing side. I strongly believe that this plan is feasible, can be implemented peacefully, and most importantly, it's "constitutional."

The fact that there are states suing the federal government, and the federal government suing the states on the two largest issues of the day, speaks volumes. When two entities that are supposed to be "married" in governance are suing each other, it's time for a divorce decree, don't you think?

My expertise is not in publishing. However, I do have over thirty years experience as an entrepreneur, an international businessman, and have extensive involvement in public affairs. My detailed credentials, experience, and resume are provided in appendix G. Currently I have a business in the blue state of Michigan and a business in the red state of Arkansas. Both are doing equally well and I expect they will both do better if the plan suggested in this book becomes a reality. I do not have an axe to grind but sincerely believe that we should all "just get along" and "live and let live."

Part I

America is Without Direction

Chapter 1

Our Great Nation is Divided

"A wise and frugal government, which shall leave men free to regulate their own pursuits of industry and improvement, and shall not take from the mouth of labor the bread it has earned - this is the sum of good government."

-Thomas Jefferson

"There can be no equality or opportunity if men and women and children be not shielded in their lives from the consequences of great industrial and social processes which they cannot alter, control, or singly cope with."

-Woodrow Wilson

"The current and expanding division within the United States is not simply a difference between Republicans and Democrats, Conservatives & Liberals, and Capitalists & Socialists etc. It is currently an irresolvable difference of opinion as to the authority and direction of our federal government. This is why there is such a polarization among the vast majority of people who have different beliefs for the present and future governance of America. The bipartisanship of the past has deteriorated to open disrespect of opposing views."

– Bob Jackson

"The terms Red states and Blue states came into use in 2000 to refer to those states of the United States whose residents predominantly vote for the Republican Party or Democrat Party presidential candidates, respectively. A Blue state tends to vote for the Democrat Party, and a Red state tends to vote for the Republican Party, although the colors were often reversed or different colors used before the 2000 election. According to AlterNet and The Washington Post, the terms were coined by journalist Tim Russert, during his televised coverage of the 2000 presidential election. That was not the first election during which the news media used colored maps to graphically depict voter preferences in the various states, but it was the first time a standard color scheme took hold. Since 2000, usage of the term has been expanded to differentiate between states being perceived as liberal and those perceived as conservative."

It is obvious to most Americans that our federal government is out of control. It is also obvious to most Americans that we are a nation divided and the division is getting more apparent as time goes on. One important fact is that President Obama has declared that his election by the Blue states was a mandate that all of America should be fundamentally changed. However, the Red states still believe that the American government is fundamentally the greatest form of government that the world has ever known. Instead of a fundamental change in the federal government, Red states believe that the country will progress and grow to the benefit of all Americans if the federal government should conform to the principles that are literally defined in the Constitution of the United States.

It is always risky to make generalizations as there are so many exceptions to every generalization that most generalizations have no value. However, in this case, the details of the daily and ongoing federal government's actions make it difficult to see the real overall situation. That said, it is generally agreed that the fundamental difference of opinion that is dividing this country is that half of the country demands an expanded federal government to move the country forward, and the other half of the country demands a smaller federal government to move the country forward. To further take advantage of generalizations, Red states generally demand an appreciably smaller federal government and the Blue states demand a significantly expanded federal government. Appendix A illustrates the generally defined Red and Blue states.

The basic problem that faces America, as I see it, is not the difference in political philosophy between the Red states and the Blue states, but is the quest for each faction to dominate the other faction. This passionate and unrelenting quest for dominance by one faction over the other is the driving force that is dividing this great country. The natural result of this pursuit of dominance will, again, in my opinion, result in a continuous deterioration of this country which will lower the standard of living for all Americans now and for future generations. Not to be trite, but the old fable of a frog that will not jump out of the pot as the water is gradually raised to a boil applies today. At what point does the population decide that enough is enough and that divisive struggle for philosophical domination through political power will destroy the government we feel passionate about? This government destruction applies equally to those who believe in Red state principles and those who believe in Blue state principles.

The division between the Blue states and the Red states also goes far beyond what has been defined as "bipartisan." Bipartisan applies when different sides negotiate for a common goal. Common goals are all too far apart between the people that agree with Red state principles and the people that agree with Blue state ideals and goals. It is also not resolvable when half the country believes passionately in one philosophy, and the other half is committed to the exact opposite philosophy.

One only needs to consider the two ideas of Obama Care (specifically the Patient Protection and Affordable Care Act and Health Care and Reconciliation Act of 2010 are hereafter in this book referred to as "Obama Care") and a balanced federal budget to understand that there is a basic polarization within this country with nearly equal numbers of passionate supporters for opposing views. There are many more basic differences between people that believe in Red state principles and Blue state principles.

The following is a list of a few of the basic beliefs of the vast majority of people that live in Red states, as shown on in appendix A:

- People with Red thoughts believe that the cornerstone of the country is the strong extended family, personal moral accountability, and only enough government to provide for domestic security and a strong national defense.

- People with Red thoughts truly believe that they could institute their corrections to the federal government and "save" the country if it was not for the obstructionist position of the Blue people.
- People with Red thoughts believe that the services and entitlements from the federal government should be significantly reduced and primary control be given back to the individual states. Many consider that this reduction should cut more than half of the current federal government services and entitlements.
- People with Red thoughts believe that the federal government should live within a balanced budget exceeded only for imminent national defense.
- Red people believe in free and open competition in the marketplace with minimum government interference. Also they believe that individuals that bring better products to the market at a lower cost can keep the profits of their hard work and investments.
- Obama Care would be abolished and health care would be reformed with state, local, and private sector improvements.
- People with Red thoughts would openly express that the foundation of the country was, and should be, based on Judeo-Christian beliefs with tolerance for all religions. The only exception would be objection to any religion that demands the overthrow of the government and non-tolerance through force against non-believers.

The following is a list of a few of the basic beliefs of the vast majority of people that live in Blue states as shown on in Appendix A:

- People with Blue thoughts believe that a strong central government is needed to provide for maximum equal opportunity for all citizens. Equal opportunity will empower the most contribution from all citizens and all citizens would be assured equal access to all the benefits produced. This is the framework that assures the most equitable domestic tranquility and distribution of wealth among the citizens.

- Blue thinking people believe that they could institute their corrections to the federal government and "save" the country if it was not for the obstructionist position of the Red people. Full implementation of Obama Care is a prime example of what the Blue states would do if there was no opposition from the Red states.

- Blue thought is not simply "tax the rich and give to the poor" as characterized by Red thought, but that it is actually the best way to build a national economy. The government should have control over the allocation of the assets needed to build a standard of living. This will make the means for growth available to the maximum number of citizens. The more people have the means for growth the more the country will grow.

- People with Blue thoughts believe that their duly elected leaders have the responsibility to control the economy so that everyone benefits equally and that the government will help individuals overcome hard times.

- People with Blue thoughts believe that the federal government should play the major role in governance. State governments should also be controlled and guided by the federal government to assure equality among all citizens regardless of the state in which they live.

- People with Blue thoughts believe that the federal government should not be financially restrained. It is the government's ultimate obligation to service the general welfare of the citizens and defend the nation. Therefore, the government should be free to make the decisions to collect and expend funds as needed by the country. Since the government leaders are duly elected by the people, they are accountable to the people, and therefore will provide the best governance possible.

The above are not the only significant differences between Blue and Red-thinking people. There are many more, and some will be discussed later in the book; however, it is also important to emphasize that there are several very important issues in which Red-thinking people and Blue thinking people agree:

- Both people with Blue and Red thinkers truly believe that they could institute their corrections to the federal government and "save" the country if it was not for the obstructionist position of the people with opposite color thoughts; however, the equal split between the different views produces the ever increasing deadlocks and defamations.

- Red and Blue thinking people each truly believe that their respective position is strictly in accordance with the United States Constitution. This fact alone makes meaningful compromises unlikely.

- There is an ever increasing frustration over the widening disagreement of government size, purpose and direction. It is evident that the current polarized federal government will not reverse the ever increasing polarization. Therefore, Red and Blue advocates both believe that, since all their actions are solidly in compliance with the Constitution, the opposition is stupid, radical, obstructionist, etc., and worthy of being demonized to the greatest extent possible. Consequently, as we have all observed, the national polarization becomes greater and greater with time and Washington becomes even more broke and broken.

There is an ever-increasing national frustration from each citizen up through the top government officials over an ever widening disagreement on government size, purpose, and direction. It is evident that the current polarized federal government will not reverse this ever increasing polarization. It would be in the best interest of all citizens if we could all "just get along" with each other. History has shown that both Red policy and Blue policy independently can provide the citizenry with peace and security as well as to provide future generations with higher standards of living. It would be a great improvement to all citizens if both the Red-thinking people could work hard to follow their conscience without being vetoed by Blue thought, and vice versa.

It is to be noted that this book does not make a case that either the Blue or Red thought is right or wrong. Actually, both the Red and Blue thoughts have great merit. To say that one thought is wrong is to say about 150 million Americans are wrong, and again, vice versa. History has shown that well motivated people with good cause and intentions can work together for the common good. This book makes the case that Red-thinking people, without the constant interference from Blue thinking people, will change their government for the betterment of all its citizens. Also, the same is true that the Blue thinking people can and will make a better government for its people if the Red-thinking people stop interfering with Blue government progress.

The main purpose for this book is to propose a way that recognizes the polarization of our nation and to suggest a peaceful and effective means to acknowledge the differences, take action, and present a way that both Red and Blue thinking people can work for their respective futures without the disruptive divisiveness that exists today. Therefore, this book makes a case for action that will allow Blue thought and Red thought to prevail simultaneously and thrive independently from each other for the maximum benefit and progress of both thoughts.

Chapter 2

The Federal Government is Broke and Broken

"My reading of history convinces me that most bad government results from too much government."

-Thomas Jefferson

"Concentrated power has always been the enemy of liberty."

-Ronald Reagan

"The test of our progress is not whether we add more to the abundance of those who have much it is whether we provide enough for those who have little."

-Franklin D. Roosevelt

The federal government is broke. We, the taxpayers, are $14 + trillion ($14,000,000,000,000.00) in debt and adding more debt every day. There has been much discussion for reducing the growth of the debt, but no action to stop borrowing, and much less consideration is given to actually paying back the debt.   When any person, company, country, or any independent entity is in so much debt that it has to borrow more money to continue, then that entity, by common sense definition, is broke. This book could add another fifty pages explaining that this country is broke, but the simple fact is that the country is just plain broke and there is no reason to expect that to change. The basic reason nothing on the horizon will make this country a strong and solvent country again is that Washington D.C. is not only broke, it is a broken entity altogether. Washington D.C. has created the debt and is unable to correct the uncontrolled growth of a bankrupt federal government. Consequently, all the people suffer from lower income opportunities and rising costs. The federal government has stated many times in the last six years that we as a country must accept a lower standard of living for current and future generations. With a broke and dysfunctional federal government, can anyone expect a better future?

This country is so divided that rational financial discourse at the federal level is not possible. The Blue thought is that more debt is needed to meet the needs of the people since the economy cannot support itself and the people. From the 1950s through 1990, the United States had far less debt and no one was dying in the streets from neglect. Currently, the Blue thought prevails, thereby making any discussion of reducing the increase of the debt would result in all the grandmas being thrown off the proverbial cliff. The leaders of the Red thought do not appear to have any solutions to controlling the debt that would also help the Red leaders gain control of the government.

Our nation was built as a representative government with checks and balances in order to maintain a vibrant federal government where every elected representative and senator had equal access to prevent the abuse of power and to formulate laws for the benefit of the people. Our government has a system where the administrative branch implements the laws and provides services authorized by the congress and senate. A third check and balance was a supreme court whose sole responsibility was to make sure that the congress and the administrative branches conformed to the constitution. That system, sadly to say, has been abrogated so badly that the administrative branch makes more laws than congress, the supreme court is a political activist more interested in changing the constitution to fit political objectives, and the congress is a polarized group that has abdicated individual initiative in favor of power politics pitting people with Red thought against people with Blue thought, and vice versa.

Generally speaking, the Republicans represent the Red people and the Democrats represent the Blue people. Caution should be exercised when discussing the political parties as Republicans representing Red thought and

Democrats representing Blue thought. There are some Republican congressmen and senators from states where the vast majority of people endorse Blue thought and are themselves Blue thinking legislators. And again, the opposite is true for Democrat legislators located in primarily Red states. The same holds true for some of the readers of this book. Some of you are Blue thinking people in a Red state, and the opposite is true as well. However, political power in Washington D.C. is seemingly lockstep Democrat verses Republican where only the leadership of each party determines the fate of the country.

The only objective of the three branches of government today is to tip the balance of power slightly in order to gain control of the government. Once in control, the Democrat forces try to force their beliefs on the Republicans, and vice versa. The reason this condition feeds upon itself is that the country is split almost evenly between Red-thinking people and Blue thinking people and neither political party can gain clear control. In 2012 the country will see over $2 billion spent on the presidential election alone to determine who will have political power. Power that will further divide this country as the winning Republican or Democrat will use the power of the presidency to force their beliefs on the opposite party, and likewise upon the opposite thinking people.

It is of great importance to this book's presentation to point out that almost all states will not be involved in electing the next president. The Red states will mostly stay Red and most of the Blue states will remain Blue. At best, the election will be decided on less than five of the fifty states. These are the ones commonly referred to as "swing" states. The philosophical differences between Republicans and Democrats are so vast that there are no negotiations – only power politics. Power politics after the 2012 election will see either the Democrats continuing to force unpopular laws on the Red states, or the Republicans forcing the Blue states to comply with Red policies. Bush tax cuts and Obama Care are prime examples of the divisive legislation from power politics. Taxing job providers versus balancing the budget will certainly be hot issues in 2013. The 2012 election, in my opinion, actually will further divide the people of this country.

Congressional politics are even more dismal looking into the future. There are 535 representatives and senators in Washington D.C. The 2010 elections were very contentious and Republicans won major victories, but did the people win? Of the 535 representatives and senators, only about ninety seats were contested. All the others were in "safe" seats. Almost all safe seats have a common characteristic: in their constituent districts, the vast majority of the voters are either Red thinking or Blue thinking people and their elected representatives and senators reflect same thought. These safe seats have yet another characteristic that is more important: repeated reelection builds seniority in the congress and senate. This seniority is the only way to rise to, and inevitably attain, political power. Consequently the leadership, as determined by seniority, are all very committed to either Red or Blue thought and not flexible to new ideas from the opposing thought leaders. The current system assures us all that parochial politics will prevail in the future with even more divisive polarization of government to continue.

Note that in 2012 there will only be, again, about ninety seats in contest. That means that more than eighty percent of the elected officials will return to office uncontested. There will be billions of dollars spent on the ninety remaining elections to convince about five percent of the people in each district to change their vote from the last election. This equates to less than one percent (five of the twenty percent contested seats) of the voting population is all that is needed to change the balance of power in Washington D.C. That is a lot of money to spend to convince such a small number of people to vote differently. This country is, indeed, divided ideologically with less than one percent of the people determining which political party will wield power.

A very good case can be made that current Washington D.C. politics are run by an elite group of only fifteen people, herein referred to as the "elite Fifteen." These leaders are given power by the seniority system and every two years there may be some change in the membership of this elite power. From 2008 to 2010 all these powerful people were all Democrats that were also strong Blue thinking people. None of the Fifteen had a mixture of Red and Blue thinking. Therefore, for two years, Blue sympathetic laws and regulations were the only products of the Washington D.C. government. This total Blue thought implementation led to an enormous growth in the size of and control of the federal government. None of the Red-thinking legislators, who comprised over forty percent of the elected people in Washington D.C., had any say in governance during this time. The utter frustration by the Red-thinking legislators and their actions to obstruct all Blue legislation produced nothing positive and strongly increased the philosophical divide in this country.

From 2010 to the time this book was published, about one-third of the elite Fifteen are Red-thinking leaders and two-thirds are Blue thinking leaders. The new third of the elite are Republicans, who, like their Democrat counterparts, are all from safe seats of Red-thinking districts. Also common to all the elite legislators, Democrats and Republicans alike, is that they all have very long seniority in Washington D.C. There is a common thought among the general public that after twenty years in Washington D.C. and "drinking Potomac water," legislators become brain dead to the desires and needs of the country in general their districts in particular. This is why it is completely understandable why congress has the approximately twenty percent approval rating from the general public. Tragically, none of the Fifteen is compassionate for, or open to, any compromise to blend Blue and Red principles to unite this great country under one prevailing set of ideals, laws, and principles. There is, in fact, open verbal warfare by both sides to demonize all opposing views and the people themselves that espouse any opposing views.

One can easily recognize that the largest issues in Washington D.C. are perpetually increasing the divide in America between Red and Blue beliefs and principles. By its nature and performance every important issue is polarized specifically on party lines and generally on Red versus Blue thought philosophy. For example, if entitlements are reduced, all grandmas will be perceived as being thrown off the proverbial cliff in wheel chairs by evil Red people. Abortion is demanded by Blue people and abhorred as murder by Red people. Tax the rich and redistribution of the wealth is demanded by the Blue people and rejected by the Red people. Working hard, growing a business, hiring people and keeping what is earned is, according to Red people, is the way to raise the standard of living for all people. The opposite is espoused by the Blue people who strongly believe that redistribution of wealth creates demand of goods and thereby increases the standard of living for all. Red people believe that a strong two parent family is the cornerstone of a free society. Blue people believe that it takes a village and strong government to develop the next generation to be the greatest it can be. The list goes on and on, and I'll discuss some other issues that relate to this point later in the book. In short, bipartisan comprise is hopelessly unobtainable as both sides want to force their principles on the other side regardless of the further national division or the demands of the general public. Washington D.C., by definition, is "broken" because it continues to divide this country without giving any indication that there will be any improvement.

With all the divisive examples aside, let's get back to the original point. The elite Fifteen that controls Washington D.C. is best defined by the offices they hold, but better recognized by the people that occupy the fifteen offices that control all actions of the federal government. The fifteen offices consist of: three in administration, six in the U.S. Senate, and six in the House of Representatives. These offices, and the current occupants, are discussed below. The resume of each of these individuals is also presented as it generally appears on each person's web page and office information material.

First, the president of the United States is, by general agreement, the most powerful person in Washington D.C. and generally accepted as the head of the Fifteen elite being discussed herein. The resume of President Obama is not as extensive as many other world and U.S. leaders. He is an attorney with about six years as a community organizer, a lackluster record as an Illinois State Senator and U.S. Senator.

Second, the secretary of state is very influential for most domestic and foreign affairs representing the United States. Secretary Hillary Clinton is also an attorney with a questioned private practice in Arkansas. She was first lady in Arkansas with eight years as first lady of the U.S. with "Hillary Care" being her most recognized activity. She also served as a strong Senator from New York for six years.

The third of the Administrative elite is the presidents chief of staff. Currently, this person is Bill Daley and he the chief advisor and scheduler to President Obama.

The twelve elite that are in addition to the three administrative elite above are members of the House and the Senate. It is important to note that no legislation is voted on in either the Senate or the House unless permitted by, and promoted by, a committee chairman. The majority leader of both chambers decides what legislation will be considered and what committee will take up the legislation.

Two of the remaining elite Fifteen are the house party leaders. The majority party leader controls the house. The minority party leader is the representative of the minority party whose primary goal is to get the minority party to lockstep oppose the vast majority of the actions of the majority party. Majority leader John Boehner has a business degree, twelve years experience controlling a private plastics business, and twenty years as a representative from Ohio. Minority leader Nancy Pelosi has a Bachelor of Science degree from Trinity College where she graduated in 1962 with very limited private business or service experience reported on her web page. She has twenty-four years of experience as a representative from California with four years as a former majority leader.

Further, there are four elite committee chairs in the House of Representatives that control most of the activities in the House. These four committees are Appropriations, Budget, Judiciary, and Energy and Commerce Committees.

Harold Rogers chairs the House Appropriations committee. The Appropriations committee is widely recognized by political scientists as one of the "power committees," since it holds the power of the purse. Openings on the Appropriations committee are often hotly demanded, and are doled out as rewards. It is one of the exclusive committees of the house, meaning its members typically sit on no other committee. Under house rules, an exception to this is that five members of the Appropriations Committee must serve on the House Budget Committee—three from the majority party and two for the minority party. Much of the power of the committee comes from the inherent utility of controlling spending. Its subcommittee chairmen are often called "cardinals" because of the power they wield over the budget. Chairman Rogers earned a LL.B law degree in 1964, and has been a representative from Kentucky for thirty years. His web page does not expound on any pre-congressional experience.

Paul Ryan chairs the House Budget Committee. Throughout its history, the Budget Committee has fulfilled its role as an institutional check on federal spending in two ways: first, the committee has consistently provided independent analyses of federal spending through the Congressional Budget Office. Second, the committee negotiates with its counterparts in the executive branch and the Senate. As a result of the institutional reforms that created the Budget Committee, congress strengthened its hand in shaping the budget and appropriations process. Chairman Ryan has a degree in Economics and Political Science and has been a representative from Wisconsin for thirteen years. Like Congressman Rodgers, his web page does not expound on any pre-congressional experience.

Lamar Smith chairs the House Judiciary Committee. The Judiciary Committee has been called the "Guardian of the Constitution." As Chairman, Congressman Smith helps shape legislation on such subjects as terrorism, crime, immigration, bankruptcy, civil liberties, constitutional amendments, patents, and copyrights. Over 1,000 bills and resolutions were referred to the House Judiciary Committee in the last congress. Chairman Smith has a law degree and experience in private practice before being elected to the House of Representatives in 1987, which would give him twenty-four years of seniority

Fred Upton chairs the House Energy and Commerce Committee. This committee writes legislation about interstate and foreign commerce, energy generation and conservation, travel and tourism, and consumer protection. This committee covers a vast amount of legislation including six powerful subcommittees including public health and the oversight of agencies, departments, and programs. Chairman Upton has a degree in Journalism and office experience in the Office of Management and Budget Department while Ronald Reagan was president. Chairman Upton has twenty-four years of seniority in Congress representing Michigan.

That completes the list of the six of the Fifteen elite that are members of the House of Representatives. Now, let's take a look at the six of the Fifteen elite that reside in the senate. Two of whom are the majority and minority party leaders. The other four are chairmen of the most powerful committees.

First, Harry Reid is the Senate Majority Leader and the most powerful person in the U.S. Senate. He decides what legislation and actions will be considered for passage by the senate and what legislation, and other activities, will not be considered. He also has great control as to who will get committee chair positions. Senator Reid was a city attorney with about three years of private practice experience before becoming a professional politician representing the state of Nevada. He was elected to the Nevada state assembly and has been a career politician since 1968. He was a U.S. Congressman through 1982, then moved on to gain thirty years of seniority as a U.S. Senator.

Second, the Senate Minority Leader is Mitch McConnell. His job is to get the minority party to lockstep oppose the vast majority of the actions of the majority party. Mitch McConnell is an attorney who served as Judge-Executive of Jefferson County, Kentucky, from 1978 until he commenced his Senate term in 1985. Senator McConnell has twenty-six years as a U.S. Senator from the state of Kentucky.

Next, there are four committee chairs in the senate that control nearly all of the senate's activities. These committees are 1. Appropriations, 2. Judiciary, 3. Banking, Housing, and Urban Affairs, and 4. Health Education Labor and Pensions. No legislation is taken up in the senate unless it is approved and released by the chairperson of each of these committees. These elite chairpersons are as follows:

Daniel Inouye is the chairman of the Appropriation Committee. The Senate Appropriations Committee is the largest committee in the U.S. Senate, consisting of thirty members in the 111th Congress. Its role is defined by the U.S. Constitution, which requires "appropriations made by law" prior to the expenditure of any money from the federal treasury. The committee writes the legislation that allocates federal funds to the numerous government agencies, departments, and organizations on an annual basis. Appropriations are limited to the levels set by a Budget Resolution drafted by the Senate Budget Committee. Chairman Inouye is a WWII veteran and he is a Medal of Honor recipient, thereby earning the highest honor of this country. He has been an elected official since 1954 with the last thirty-six years as a senator representing the state of Hawaii.

Patrick Leahy is the chairman of the Senate Judiciary Committee. The Judiciary Committee is the most powerful committee in the Senate. It provides oversight of the Department of Justice and the agencies under the Department's jurisdiction, including the Federal Bureau of Investigation, and the Department of Homeland Security. The Senate Judiciary Committee validates or rejects supreme court nominations, appellate court nominations, district court nominations, and a multitude of the executive branch nominations. In addition, the Senate Judiciary Committee also considers a major portion of Senate legislation, resolutions, messages, petitions, memorials, and other matters. Chairman Leahy has been an attorney since 1964, and has been a U.S. Senator from the State of Vermont for thirty-seven years. His web page does not expound on any pre-congressional experience.

Tim Johnson is the Chairman of the Senate Banking, Housing, and Urban Affairs Committee. This committee has jurisdiction over matters related to banks, price controls, deposit insurance, exports, federal monetary policy, financial aid to commerce and industry, issuance of currency and coinage, public and private housing, urban development, mass transit, and government contracts. Chairman Johnson has a law degree from the University of South

Dakota. He was a private attorney from 1975 through 1978. Since 1987 he has been a professional politician for the state of South Dakota as a state house representative from 1978 to 1982, a state senator from 1982 to 1986, a U.S. Congressman from 1986 to 1996, and a U.S. Senator for fifteen years.

Finally, Tom Harkin is the chairman of the Senate Committee on Health, Education, Labor and Pensions. Even though this committee, in my opinion, ranks fourth in Senate power, this committee has a very far reaching jurisdiction. According to Wikipedia the committee covers:

- Measures relating to education, labor, health, and public welfare
- Aging
- Agricultural colleges
- Arts and humanities
- Biomedical research and development
- Child labor
- Convict labor and the entry of goods made by convicts into interstate commerce
- Domestic activities of the American Red Cross
- Equal employment opportunity
- Gallaudet University, Howard University, and St. Elizabeth's Hospital in Washington D.C.
- Individuals with disabilities
- Labor standards and labor statistics
- Mediation and arbitration of labor disputes
- Occupational Safety and Health Administration
- Mine Safety and Health Administration
- Private pension plans
- Public health
- Railway labor and retirement

- Regulation of foreign laborers
- Student loans
- Wages and hours of labor, including the federal minimum wage

Chairman Senator Tom Harkin has service in the Navy as a pilot followed by earning a law degree. He has represented Iowa in Washington D.C. for thirty-six years. From 1974 through 1984 he was a U.S. Congressman. He is now a senator from Iowa with twenty-six years of seniority.

The information for the elite Fifteen leaders in Washington D.C. above shows almost complete control of Washington D.C. that cannot and will not be challenged in the foreseeable future. There are some very troubling common traits that could explain why Washington D.C. is broken. For example, the vast majority of the Fifteen are attorneys with very limited legal experience in the private sector. That wouldn't be alarming except attorneys are trained to define differences and use parochial issues instead of common facts to determine winners and losers. They are trained to polarize issues and not to find common ground.

Also, there is almost no real-life experience among the Fifteen. None were great leaders outside Washington D.C. with extensive experience in business, legal, educational, labor, social, or any other major American endeavor. Additionally, all are from safe political districts that have significant majorities that are either Red or Blue thinking people, without enough oppositional thought to challenge them. Therefore, all of the Fifteen elite were already polarized as Red or Blue long before they were elevated to power.

The Seniority system has created the real dysfunction in Washington D.C. Why is it that no experienced and proven leaders from the private sector are in congress or the senate? Why won't proven leaders run for congress and the senate? Leaders like Bill Gates, Jesse Jackson, Donald Trump, George

Soros, Jimmy Hoffa, Ross Perrot, Bill Ayres, Steve Jobs, and at least a million other achievers that have better proven experience than any of the representatives, or senators in general, and the Fifteen elite in particular? The answer is that they simply will not commit at least twenty years of their time following the elite leaders in lockstep in order to get to a position where they could use their expertise. About twenty years ago many states voted for, and instituted, term limits so that more qualified candidates could be attracted to political office. The legislation included term limits for representatives and senators. History has shown that term limits did produce better legislators that were more attuned with their states' needs and desires. The elite Washington D.C. power pressed the Supreme Court to say that the voted will of the people was insufficient to breach the power of the elite Fifteen. In my opinion, a term limit constitutional amendment alone will neither correct the federal government's dysfunction, nor will Washington D.C. ever formulate a term limit amendment on its own.

Thus, congress will not change with future elections. In 2010 it was assumed that there was a major redirection of the government as the Republicans gained a large majority in the House of Representatives. However, less than twenty percent of the congress members were changed, none received any chair of any committee, and over half the new members followed lockstep with the leadership in order to get better office allocation and meaningful committee assignments. Ten percent of new representatives will not change the direction of an entrenched congress in general, and the elite Fifteen will not allow the changes expected by the voters. The senate was less affected by 2010 elections. I expressed my concern over the 2010 election in an openly published letter to the editor:

November 14, 2010

Ref: New Congress Expectations

Dear Editor,

Wow, we now have a new Congress and we will get a lot of new changes. Or will it be business as usual?

There are about 85 new incoming congressmen in the 435 member House. Therefore, about eighty percent of Congress still consists of Potomac water saturated big government incumbents. In order to get good committee assignments, perks and offices the new members must pledge lock step allegiance to a leadership with each having twenty-five plus years seniority. At least half of the freshmen will succumb to Washington D.C. politics leaving only about ten percent of new congressmen with true change on their minds.

What would real change look like? Eliminate some departments completely. In the 1950's the US had the best education system in the world with no Washington D.C. mandates. Now we are below the world average. By eliminating the department of education we would save significant federal spending and return education to the states and locals. Really, parents are more concerned with the education of their children than Washington D.C.. Also the current anti-capitalism, politically correct and socialistic mandates would be removed from our children's diet.

Want to balance the budget? How about lowering the poverty level ceiling for all entitlements to $20,000 per year for both single and married households, citizens only? This way the truly needy citizens will be fully assisted at huge savings and two parent families will get equal treatment. Remember that $20,000 per year is in the top five percent of the world's pay scale and Obama wants the US to downgrade our standard of living to be in line with world needs.

More change? It is acknowledged that federal employees are paid thirty percent more than the comparable tax-paying public. Our federal employees' only mandate is to redistribute tax-payer money with none of the competitive pressures that applies to taxpayers. Let's be fair. Federal pay should be returned to 2006 levels and held constant until federal pay is equal to comparable private pay. Does equal pay for equal work ring a bell?

Has Washington D.C. suggested such significant changes that would actually reduce the size of government and balance a budget? Do you really expect big change? How about term limits to change the leadership to get real change?

Yours Truly

Robert Jackson

New representatives and senators learn early on that they need to build seniority and support the leadership in order to ever have a chance to affect governance. While congressmen and senators build seniority, their main concern is reelection. Financial resources are critical for repeated reelections and that changes the allegiance from the citizens to the lobbyists and special interest groups. Political alliances are also critical to multiple reelections. Both of the above situations lead to "pay to play" and expanded government to increase benefits to the lobby and special interest groups, for example. During this process the elected official must show they are really Blue thinking if their district is Blue and truly Red-thinking if their district is Red. This is inherently a flawed process.

It is also important to reflect on the Supreme Court and federal courts in order to holistically evaluate Washington D.C. The Supreme Court, federal appeals court, and federal courts are becoming more polarized and are building a reputation for "legislating form the bench" instead of strictly ruling on the constitutionality of the issues brought before to courts. Because Red thoughts and the Blue thoughts are diametrically opposed on the important issues, the function of the supreme court is seriously undermined and is becoming a force that further polarizes the country. This will only get worse in coming years. The recommendation put forth in this book should reestablish the supreme court as a true arm of the constitutional "check and balance" system of government, where it properly belongs.

Therefore, Washington D.C. is broken. It is duly disrespected by about eighty percent of Americans, and it has proven that it will not make any structural changes for the common good of all Americans. The elite Fifteen covet political power for powers sake and will continue to expand its power. Washington D.C. will not change. If Americans want change they can believe in, they must use their constitutional power and make Washington D.C. change against its will. The good news is that it can happen that way. That is the crux of this book. There is a way to restructure national government to better serve the people without needing Washington D.C. to do it for us.

Chapter 3

Future Alternatives for America

"A democracy is always temporary in nature; it simply cannot exist as a permanent form of government. A democracy will continue to exist up until the time that voters discover that they can vote themselves generous gifts from the public treasury. From that moment on, the majority always votes for the candidates who promise the most benefits from the public treasury, with the result that every democracy will finally collapse over loose fiscal policy, (which is) always followed by a dictatorship."

"The average age of the world's greatest civilizations from the beginning of history, has been about 200 years. During those 200 years, these nations always progressed through the following sequence:

From bondage to spiritual faith;
From spiritual faith to great courage;
From courage to liberty;
From liberty to abundance;
From abundance to complacency;
From complacency to apathy;
From apathy to dependence;
From dependence back into bondage."

In 1887 Alexander Tyler, a Scottish history professor at the University of Edinborough, said this about the fall of the Athenian Republic some 2,000 years prior.

It is a common belief by about eighty percent of Americans that Washington D.C. is both broke and broken. If left unchanged, Washington D.C. will drag down the American standard of living now and into the future...'nuff said! I'm sure that most of us either currently enjoy our standard of living, or are working diligently to improve the standard we now have. Therefore, the reality of seeing Washington D.C. destroy what we've worked so hard to build is not acceptable. What alternatives are available that will make enough difference to make a difference? Let's carefully examine our options.

The easiest alternative is to just let things progress as they have been. Actually, we really do not have to do anything. Complete apathy. Just like a frog in a pan on the stove that doesn't have to jump out as the temperature rises slowly; however, we all know how that story ends for the frog! Think of how frustrating it is to see the growing division in America between the Democrat and Republican parties. Doesn't it make you want to turn off the television sometimes? The Democrat leadership, as previously explained, consists of solidly Blue committed people who are committed to forcing Blue governance on all Americans. Likewise, the Republican leadership is committed to forcing Red ideas on all Americans. There is no indication that the division will ever close with current Washington D.C. politics, or that any real "bipartisan compromise" will ultimately be achieved. To make matters even worse, the federal government is growing at an accelerated rate which increases the power of the leadership on both sides. Most political analysts agree that continuation of the status quo will result in an irreversible total economic collapse. Thus, all we need to do as a country is be happy in our complacency and we'll experience exactly what is coming to us, without having to lift a single finger.

Another alternative, especially of interest to some of the Blue thinking Americans known as the "far left," is to recognize that the current government will collapse, and the sooner it collapses, the sooner a totally new government can be established. They see this new government as totally Blue in direction with the federal government directly helping all Americans to ensure that all the people's needs are fairly and equitably met. This alternative has several large advantages. For example, all unfunded pension debt, both public and private, will simply disappear and not be needed as the new government will take care of all retired senior citizens equally through fairly implemented social entitlement programs. Additionally, health care will also not be a problem. Everyone will have government supplied health care regardless of the causes for the health care need. It would not matter if the care is a result of an occupational accident, public accident, illness, old age, preexisting condition, or any reason at all. Everyone would get the care they need free from the government. This new government, duly elected by and responsible to the public, would also manage the production of goods so that the priorities of the public needs can best be met with excessive corporate profits taxed to support the government entitlement services. It is also noteworthy that some of the Red-thinking Americans, known as the "far right," likewise believe that the current government will collapse, and the sooner the better. They strongly believe that the new government would be strictly constitutionalist in nature, like the founding fathers originally intended, and there would be a very small central government that would institute Red ideas. Is it not strange that opposite thinking people see things completely differently?

The current and most aggressively sought after direction for the federal government is what we see every day, and has the support of most Americans. This alternative is centered on either the Republicans or Democrats having prolonged control of the presidency, fifty-one percent of congress, fifty-one percent of the senate, and the majority of the supreme court. If the Republicans gain this total federal government control, then America would turn sharply to a Red based society. All citizens would therefore be required to obey laws and regulations based on Red philosophy and ideals. The same holds true if the Democrats win total control for a long time America will become a completely Blue-based society. The main difficulty of this future for America is that just fewer than fifty percent of the people will be forced to live in a society that is abhorrent to their own personal, religious, political, and patriotic beliefs.

How many people realize how much disruption over forty percent of the population can cause when they truly believe that they are being forced to comply with a completely unjust country, in their eyes?

"To compel a man to furnish funds for the propagation of ideas he disbelieves and abhors is sinful and tyrannical."
-Thomas Jefferson

Idealists see another path for America. They see that the divided Red and Blue philosophies will find a way to compromise their core values and we will all merge into an effective government. The catch words like "bipartisan" and "compromise" are the methods they see as working in the future. Has anyone seen any actions in this direction? It reminds me of two phrases: "Drink my Kool-Aid and all will be better," and "I have a bridge in Brooklyn to sell you." Maybe this path will hold a beneficial and healing future for America, but I for one am not holding my breath.

There is a good case to be made that term limits would have a very positive effect to repair a broken Washington D.C. There are three main reasons for this major impact: First, there would be better qualified candidates seeking office and being elected. Secondly, the absolute power gridlock over Washington D.C. by the elite Fifteen leaders of either major party would be broken and more legislators would be given an opportunity to shape the government as desired by their districts. Third, and arguably most significant, the elected representatives and senators would nearly all return, after serving their term, to their prior avocations, knowing they will have to live under the laws and regulations they enact. In other words, they will not be exempt from any new laws they helped to create.

Consider this as an example of the legislative process if congress was limited to five two-year terms, or ten years in all: For the first two terms, the newly elected representative will need to represent their districts effectively at the national level and demonstrate competence in order to get reelected. The third term would add the responsibility of melding their district's needs into national initiatives and learn the intimate workings of the committees. The last two terms would both permit and require the representative to lead one or more committees in the formation of new laws, adjustment of prior laws, and even repealing laws and regulations found to be lacking in performance. Then the representative would return to the district and live under the government they helped to shape. There are multitudes of web pages and organizations that are deeply involved with the term limit issue. The reader should be encouraged to further inquire about term limits on the web.

Fifteen states have passed legislation, or state constitutional amendments, for term limits for state lawmakers. However, state supreme courts have voided term limit provisions in Massachusetts, Oregon, Washington and Wyoming. Also, two of the fifteen states who passed term limit legislation, Idaho and Utah, have subsequently repealed their term limit requirements for their state legislatures. Therefore, only nine states representing both Blue and Red states currently have term limits for their state legislatures. Several of these states also passed laws and amendments for term limits for representatives and senators which were all ruled unconstitutional by the U.S. supreme court in May of 1995 in the Thornton decision. Further rationale for the belief behind the effectiveness of term limits can be explained through my personal experience working in Michigan politics.

I have over thirty years of experience as an entrepreneur and businessman in Michigan, and I also have political experiences before and after term limits were instituted in Michigan. appendix G at the end of this book contains my complete resume. In the early 1980s, the Michigan house had a few well-entrenched, long seniority, legislators that controlled all legislation. Benton Harbor was one of the most distressed cities in the United States and was in dire need for assistance in order to rebuild a decimated business community. I led the lobbying effort to revive the business climate in Benton Harbor. There was a vast majority of Benton Harbor people and those in the surrounding area that agreed on proposed legislation that would give Benton Harbor a chance to rebuild from within; however, the committee chairperson in control would not allow consideration of the proposed legislation. He demanded special consideration for his upper Michigan district as hostage for the legislation. For several years, Benton Harbor continued to suffer because of the obstinate behavior of one entrenched elite leader. "Pay for play" and "ear mark" equivalents were normal in all negotiations in order to get approval from the elite high seniority leaders. There was also great public concern that most legislators were, at best, mediocre in meeting their constituents' needs. Qualified candidates were discouraged from running for office as they knew they would need about twenty years seniority before they could affect any legislation. The main reasons for the term limit movement in Michigan, in my opinion, was that it was the only way to break the elite leader's parochial control. The movement also wanted to promote better qualified candidates for office by providing the means where all legislators had an equal opportunity to participate in Michigan's government soon after they were elected. Now, there is significant resistance to term limits for the exact opposite reason term limits were enacted. There are also a lot of very good legislators that are being termed out. Go figure.

Actually term limits for Washington D.C.'s legislators is, in all reality, a wasted discussion because the elite fifteen (chapter 2) just will not permit the destruction of their grip on their power over the government.

Another way to effectively change the power structure in Washington D.C. is for some states to secede from the United States. Not since the civil war has seccession risen to such a high fever. Most Blue leaning states believe the

civil war is over and done with. Not so in the South and many other Red states.
The only issue settled by the civil war for good, and rightfully so, was the
abolishment of slavery. The economic retribution by the North over the South
both before and after the war was so severe and arbitrary that it is still
remembered widely across the South. Most of the North is strongly Blue in its
politics, and most of the South is Red in its politics. This division is getting
wider every day the federal government grows larger and more dominant over
the everyday life of individuals. One clear troubling example is Obama Care.
About twenty-seven states have united in a lawsuit aimed at abolishing Obama
Care as unconstitutional. There will be no winners in this case. If it is ruled
constitutional, the Blue people will rejoice and the nearly equal number of Red
people will be very angry. The Red people will not say "oh well we will joyously
accept the supreme court decision." And, naturally, if the supreme court rules
Obama Care to be unconstitutional, the Blue people will be angry, and angry
people do not act rationally. This issue alone could be the tipping point of
complete separation of any commonality left between Red and Blue thinking
people. The real problem with secession is that it almost always results in
violence. At the very least, it would be extremely disruptive to society, life and
property.

Finally, after all the foregoing rhetoric, comes the essence of this book.
Replace Red versus Blue with Red and Blue. There is, in my opinion, a feasible
action plan that would let the Red states and the Blue states pursue their
committed paths peaceably and independently of each other. Simply stated,
the Blue and Red states should separate from each other and form two
separate and independent soverign countries.   The United States Constitution
is probably the best political document the world has seen for over 200 years.
It has one unique feature that allows for a controlled adjustment to changing
times. There have been twenty-seven amendments to the constitution that

have kept it current with the times. Now is the time to consider the biggest amendment ever contemplated. We should consider an amendment that would separate the United States into two independent and sovereign countries. Each would agree to adopt the current United States Constitution, amendments, existing laws and regulations, and other current government activities. Once implemented, each country will be free to interpret and amend their constitution as their constitution permits without the interference of the other similarly established country. One country would consist of the predominately Blue states and the other country consisting of the predominately Red states. The philosophy of "live and let live" is not all bad. The next chapter outlines a possible format for such an amendment followed by chapters outlining the transition and consequences of such a massive change.

Article V of the Constitution specifies that the people shall amend the constitution when needed to preserve the liberty, freedom, and general welfare of the people.

Part II

A New Course for America

Chapter 4

The Next Amendment to the Constitution

"All persons ought to endeavor to follow what is right, and not what is established."

- Aristotle

The objective of this book is to show the reader that an amendment to the U.S. Constitution is the best way to fix a broke and broken federal government and also the best way to heal the ever increasing divide among the people of this country. This course of action is the only plan that will peacefully allow blue thinking people to determine the future of their government without the interference of diametrically opposed red-thinking people, and vice versa. "Live and let live" is a good policy, and this proposed amendment would implement just that. The following is Article V of the U.S. Constitution:

Article V of the Constitution of the United States - Amendment

http://www.usconstitution.net/const.html#Article5

The Congress, whenever two-thirds of both Houses shall deem it necessary, shall propose Amendments to this Constitution, or, on the application of the Legislatures of two-thirds of the several States, shall call a Convention for proposing Amendments, which, in either case, shall be valid to all intents and purposes, as part of this Constitution, when ratified by the Legislatures of three-fourths of the several States, or by Conventions in three-fourths thereof, as the one or the other mode of ratification may be proposed by the Congress; provided that no Amendment which may be made prior to the year One Thousand Eight Hundred and Eight shall in any manner affect the first and fourth clauses in the Ninth Section of the first Article; and that no State, without its consent, shall be deprived of its equal suffrage in the Senate.

The Amendment Process

http://www.usconstitution.net/constam.html#process 7-23-11

There are essentially two ways spelled out in the Constitution for how to propose an amendment. One has never been used.

The first method is for a bill to pass both houses of the legislature, by a two-thirds majority in each. Once the bill has passed both houses, it goes on to the states. This is the route taken by all current amendments. Because of some long outstanding amendments, such as the 27th, Congress will normally put a time limit (typically seven years) for the bill to be approved as an amendment (for example, see the 21st and 22nd).

The second method prescribed is for a Constitutional Convention to be called by two-thirds of the legislatures of the States, and for that Convention to propose one or more amendments. These amendments are then sent to the states to be approved by three-fourths of the legislatures or conventions. This route has never been taken, and there is discussion in political science circles about just how such a convention would be convened, and what kind of changes it would bring about.

Regardless of which of the two proposal routes is taken, the amendment must be ratified, or "approved," by three-fourths of the states. There are two ways to do this. The text of the amendment may specify whether the bill must be passed by the state legislatures or by a state convention. Amendments are sent to the legislatures of the states by default. Only one amendment, the 21st, specifies a convention. In any case, passage by the legislature or convention is by simple majority.

The constitution then spells out four paths for an amendment:

1. Proposal by convention of states, ratification by state conventions (never used)
2. Proposal by convention of states, ratification by state legislatures (never used)
3. Proposal by Congress, ratification by state conventions (used once)
4. Proposal by Congress, ratification by state legislatures (used all other times)

It is interesting to note that at no point does the president have a role in the formal amendment process (though he would be free to make his opinion known). He cannot veto an amendment proposal, nor veto ratification. This point is clear in Article 5, and was reaffirmed by the supreme court in Hollingsworth v Virginia (3 US 378 [1798]):

"The negative of the president applies only to the ordinary cases of legislation: he has nothing to do with the proposition, or adoption, of amendments to the constitution."

Congress can initiate an amendment to the constitution like it has for all preceding amendments. But it needs to be acknowledged that Washington D.C. in general and the congress, in particular, are functionally broken. The elite Fifteen (chapter 2), with nearly all the power in Washington D.C., will not give up any political power. It is unrealistic to expect Washington D.C. to truly fix the problems they created; problems that empower the elite who feed on expanded government to further expand their control over the United States.

I propose that the States should follow path number two above; however, it should be absolutely made clear to the reader that this book only make suggestions for the content of the proposed amendment. It should also be made absolutely clear that the Constitutional Convention will determine the names of the two new sovereign states. I will use the terms "Blue Country" and "Red Country" as my designations for the purposes of discussion. It will be the duly convened Constitutional Convention that will create the actual proposed amendment and submit it to the states legislatures for adoption. The states can amend the constitution. To use a familiar phrase – "it's constitutional"

Proposed Constitutional Amendment
Twenty-eighth Amendment (201X)
Divide the United States of America into two sovereign states

Section 1

The United States shall be replaced in its entirety as a sovereign state with two new independent sovereign states: one being the "Blue Country" and one being the "Red Country." The new Blue Country will consist of the District of Columbia and the twenty-two current states of California, Connecticut, Delaware, Hawaii, Illinois, Indiana, Maine, Maryland, Massachusetts, Michigan, Nevada, New Hampshire, New Jersey, New York, Ohio, Oregon, Pennsylvania, Rhode Island, Vermont, Washington, west Virginia, and Wisconsin. The new Red Country shall consist of the twenty-eight current states of Alabama, Alaska, Arizona, Arkansas, Colorado, Florida, Georgia, Idaho, Iowa, Kansas, Kentucky, Louisiana, Minnesota, Mississippi, Missouri, Montana, Nebraska, New Mexico, North Carolina, North Dakota, Oklahoma, South Carolina, Tennessee, Texas, Utah, Virginia and Wyoming. The citizens of the Territories will vote for independence from, inclusion to, either of the two new sovereign countries.

Section 2

The two new sovereign states shall each adopt the current United States Constitution in its entirety including all amendments and precedents.

Section 3

No state or federal laws or precedents shall be changed by this amendment and will be in effect after the adoption of this amendment by both the Red Country and the Blue Country. The new Red Country and the new Blue Country shall, as sovereign countries, modify, interpret, and amend their respective laws and constitutions as authorized under their constitutions.

Section 4

The current federal congress, administration, and supreme court shall exist for two years after the adoption of this amendment. The only powers of the old United States government shall be to divide all the federal assets and obligations, including the military, equally between the Blue Country and the Red Country based on the population as recorded by the 2010 censes, namely forty seven percent to the Red Country and fifty three percent to the new Blue Country. Federally owned real property shall be owned by the new sovereign country in which it is located.

Section 5

Each new sovereign country will establish its own supreme court according to its own constitution. The United States Circuit Court of Appeals will continue except the states of Alaska, Montana, Idaho, and Arizona will be reassigned to the 10th District, and the states of Michigan, Ohio and west Virginia will be reassigned to the 3rd District. The federal courts will continue in the states previously authorized. Three of the current supreme court justices are to be selected for each of the new countries. The three unselected justices will retire after they adjudicate conflicts in the division of assets and obligations from the old United States to the two new countries.

Section 6

All foreign treaties and other agreements in effect at the time of the adoption of this amendment shall remain in place for both the new Blue Country and to the new Red Country. The new Blue Country and the new Red Country may renegotiate or change any foreign agreement or treaty and establish mutual treaties as independent sovereign countries.

Section 7

All citizens of the current United States shall have dual citizenship with the new Blue Country and the new Red Country for five years after the adoption of this amendment, after which they will be granted sole citizenship in the country of residence. For the same period of five years, a border state may secede from either the new Blue Country or the new Red Country and join the adjacent country by a two-thirds vote of that state's legislative bodies, and a majority of the accepting country's house and senate. Residents of non-state territories shall vote for independence or incorporation to either the new Red Country or the new Blue Country.

<u>**End of The Proposed Constitutional Amendment**</u>

The proposed amendment above conforms to two important ideals of the founding fathers of the United States. Emphasis has been added to illustrate meaning.

- The preamble to the Constitution: "We the People of the United States, in order to form a more perfect Union, establish justice, insure domestic

Tranquility, provide for the common defense, promote the general Welfare, and secure the Blessings of Liberty to ourselves and our Posterity, do ordain and establish this Constitution for the United States of America."

- The preamble to the Bill of Rights: "THE Conventions of a number of the States having at the time of their adopting the Constitution, expressed a desire, in order to prevent misconstruction or abuse of its powers, that further declaratory and restrictive clauses should be added: And as extending the ground of public confidence in the Government, will best insure the beneficent ends of its institution."

My proposed amendment is just that – a proposed amendment. In order to start the process, I propose that the governors of at least two-thirds of the states discuss a plan to call for a Constitutional Convention. The more states that participate, the better the quality of the resulting proposed amendment will be. The governors should then coordinate with their respective legislatures to call the convention and specify how the delegations to the convention would be formed. It will be very important that each state participating in the convention have equitable representation among the convention members. Some specific details could be written into the amendment such as new names for the two new countries, the specific members designated for each new country, and a time limit for passage; however, if excessive details are incorporated, the amendment becomes inflexible and unduly restrictive. The proposed amendment above would set up sufficient authorization that would allow an equitable and timely transition from the current United States into two separate sovereign countries. Later chapters of this book will be focused on how this proposed amendment will be implemented. Some chapters will be focused on the majors issues of the day, consequences, and a forecast of how these issues will evolve in the future for both the Red Country and the Blue Country.

I have been somewhat presumptuous in naming each state as Red-thinking and Blue thinking, but I believe that most if not all designations are fairly accurate based on the currently elected government officials in each state for both statewide and federal representation. The names I suggest for each new country are simply suggestions, with the actual names being determined by either the constitutional convention or later by each new country itself after the amendment is adopted. For this book, I simply refer the new country of blue leaning states as "Blue Country" and the new country of red leaning states as the "Red Country."

Chapter 5

Transition without disruption

A great advantage of the proposed amendment is that its implementation in both new countries will actually be set up in full detail by their adopted constitutions. Also, from day one, both new countries will be staffed sufficiently to make federal government transfer from the old United States almost seamless. This amendment will have miniscule effects on state governments who will continue their normal legislative agenda and services. Of great significance is that each new country will have in place, on day one, a duly elected congress and senate that conforms to their respective constitutions. The current representatives and senators simply report to a new capital and take up their elected duties. The great difference is that a large majority of the new Red Country representatives and senators will be committed to Red beliefs and principles. And a large majority of the new Blue Country federal legislature will be committed to an agenda based on Blue philosophy.

After the amendment is ratified, each of the twenty-eight states of the new Red Country will have two duly elected Senators with an already determined reelection rotation. The new Blue Country will also have two sitting senators for each state. Both new countries will also have incumbent representatives properly apportioned among all the states that were elected in conformance with the new, as well as the old, constitutions. Both the House of Representatives and Senate will be constitutionally in place and capable of conducting the full business of the new federal governments immediately after the amendment is ratified. Appendices B and C present the membership that would be in place if the amendment is ratified before the end of 2012. There may be up to a twenty percent change in house members and up to a ten percent change in the senate members after 2012 elections, but the Red and Blue make-up will experience little change.

All pre-ratification federal laws, regulations, and established precedents will apply on day one in both new sovereign states. No changes in enforcement would be expected except jurisdictions would be restricted to each new sovereign country. The current employees for the federal government are widely spread across the country with actually only a small portion in Washington D.C. In each state there are federal employees that take care of the daily duties coordinating federal laws, regulations, and services with state and local entities. It would be expected that the vast majority of current federal employees throughout the new countries would simply be rehired by the new country with jurisdiction over the state in which the employee already resides. Even though the employer would change, the duties would resume unaltered until the new country decides to change its laws. All federal entitlements such as Social Security, Medicare, and welfare, as well as federal services such as food inspection, customs, border control, immigration and the rest of the multitude of current federal services would continue uninterrupted and unchanged until the new government changes the rules and/or services within its own country. Disruptions in services, if any, would be minor. The reader is encouraged to refer to the table of contents to find chapters that cover specific issues and government functions in more detail.

State governments would not have any changes within each state. They would have the same institutional relationship with a new federal government that they had with the old government. However, the new federal government would be about one-half the size of the old federal government. The greatest advantage for state governments is that nearly all states will have a federal government that is more sympathetic to the state government and its citizens. Blue states in the Blue Country would have a federal government that has a large majority of Blue thinking legislators, administration, and court system. Conversely, Red states would also enjoy a similarly compatible federal government in the new Red Country. It would be reasonable to expect that the transition from one all-encompassing federal government to a smaller and more compatible federal government will make the transition actually easier than continuing current interactions with a broke and broken Washington D.C.

The federal court system would remain until changed by the new congresses. There would be some disruption in a few states as the circuit courts would be reassigned to new appeals courts. A ratified amendment should rearrange the appeals court jurisdictions so that all appeals courts will be fully encompassed in one of the new countries or the other. There is a transition needed for the supreme courts that is detailed in chapter 6; however, the realignment of the supreme courts can be done where no citizen, or other entity, would lose any constitutionally guaranteed legal redress.

It should be noted that all foreign treaties and contracts will remain in effect after ratification until changed by either, or both, new country. The domestic military transition can be done smoothly and it is in everyone's best interest to do so. Foreign military bases and engagements will need to be very carefully handled. At the outset, both new countries will have a common defense policy, but these policies will eventually drift apart. Even though both Red and Blue thinking people agree that a strong national defense is required, it must be recognized the there is strong disagreement as to how to best provide a strong national defense. I would, however, expect that for the foreseeable future there would be a common agreement that an attack on one country would be interpreted as an attack on the other, and both new countries would rise to a common defense. Chapter 12 discusses the military transition in more detail.

The population demographics and national boundaries for the two new countries are discussed in chapter 11. There should not be a concern with the population size of either of the two new countries. appendix E shows close to the current population of the fifteen most populated countries in the world. appendix F shows the realignment of the world population after the current United States is replaced by the new Blue Country (ranked 6th in the world) and the new Red Country (ranked 9th just above Russia at number 10). Just think: the G8 will become the G9 with Americans having two votes instead of one.

To conclude, the adoption of the current Constitution provides the way for a seamless transition in the creation of two new countries. After ratification, each independent and sovereign country can proceed to change laws and regulations in a controlled way, and completely on their own. The new Blue Country can adopt ever increasing Blue characteristics as desired by their states and citizens without the obstructionist actions by Red-thinking people, and vice versa. Through this process, both new countries can progress toward what they perceive to be the betterment of its citizens. The current broke and broken federal government will simply and peacefully fade into history. "Live and let live" is a time-proven principle of peace and prosperity for all.

Again I suggest that the reader refers to the table of contents for additional chapters in this book that discuss the transition and expected future expectations for specific issues.

Chapter 6

Implementation of the Amendment

The new legislative branches of the new Red Country and the new Blue Country will convene independently soon after the amendment is ratified. These two new countries, as empowered by the amendment, will have in place a working and complete constitution. By these constitutions each new country will have in place, day one, a complete Congress and Senate. The U.S. Congress and Senate existing before the adoption of the amendment will be dissolved upon adoption of the amendment because they will not have any authority to make any new laws or regulations on behalf of the old United States.

The prior federal legislators will be the same Congresspersons and Senators of the two new countries. All members will be the original members of the new Congresses and Senates in either the Red Country or the Blue Country depending on the states they represent. They will have already been duly elected in each state they represent and properly apportioned among the states according to the new constitutions. By existing rules, and their new constitutions, the Congresses for each new sovereign country shall determine a house speaker who will immediately become the new president in order to fill a vacancy according to the constitution. Then the house will elect a new speaker who will immediately become the new vice president. The new administration will then form a cabinet subject to the ratification of the Senate in conformance with a well established constitution. Once the new government is established, any new candidates may run for elected office, regardless of their past experience as United States politicians. For example, Bill Clinton would be an eligible candidate for the Blue Country's first official presidential election.

With the new administration in place each new sovereign country can conduct the business of state within their constitution with no regard to the other new sovereign state's actions or agenda. The new Red Country and the new Blue Country will be two independent sovereign states and shall act accordingly. The amendment provides for an immediate, duly authorized, and functional federal government for each country in a very short time. It will take some time for the states to ratify the amendment presented by the Constitutional Convention. It should be pointed out the there will be a lot of time to prepare for the formation of the two new sovereign countries. There will not be any surprises, and the details for the initial functions of government will be worked out while the amendment is in the process of ratification by the states. Additionally, some importance is placed on the old United States Congress and Senate to be dissolved upon ratification of the amendment by each new country.

For each new country, the new president, according to the constitution, shall appoint nine supreme court justices subject to senate approval. Three of the nine will be selected from the nine old United States supreme court justices according to the amendment. Six will be newly appointed justices. The intent of the founding fathers was for a supreme court whose members change infrequently. The proposed amendment would establish all nine new supreme court justices at the same time. Provisions should be made that would allow a controlled replacement of the new nine justices over time. The three selected justices from the old United States supreme court would maintain their life-long appointment. Every two years, one of the newly appointed six supreme court justices will be retired from the bench. Therefore, in eighteen years, the supreme court will consist of justices appointed in two-year intervals. The justice to be excused shall be chosen by lot among each other. The terms and conditions of all subsequent justices to be replaced after the original seven have been replaced or retired will be in accordance with the new country's constitution. This process allows justice to be administered without disruption after the amendment is adopted. It also provides a transition period so that a supreme court will be established within the letter and intent of the constitution.

This establishment process for the new supreme courts is a strong reinforcement for the need of the proposed amendment. It is very clear Red Country will select the three most conservative justices from the current supreme court as the first three of their new supreme court. It is equally apparent that Blue Country will select the most progressive three justices to join their initial supreme court. There will be no arguments over any justice being requested by each new country. This is in itself is proof-positive that the current supreme court is as divided philosophically as the current congress, senate, and administration as explained in chapter 1.

Below the supreme court are the federal courts of appeals and subordinate to the courts of appeals are the federal district courts. Federal district courts are the general trial courts of the federal court system. All federal related civil and criminal cases are first filed and adjudicated in the district court. There is also a bankruptcy court associated with each of the district courts. Each federal judicial district has at least one courthouse. There is at least one district court for each state and one for the District of Columbia. There are eighty-nine districts in the fifty States. Since the district courts are located within states, and every state has at least one district court, there will be no change or disruption in the federal court system when the proposed amendment is ratified. Since all current laws before the ratification of the amendment will be in effect after the ratification, there will be no disruption in case load or schedule for any district court in either the new Blue Country or the new Red Country. Of course, after the two new countries are formed the will be new and different laws enacted for each sovereign country. It is expected that the Blue County will add to and change their laws to be more progressive in conformance with the desires of the majority of their citizens. The new Red Country would predictably modify their laws to be more politically conservative.

Each state has a federal court system in place. Appeals from any district court decision are made with a federal appeals court. Appeals for decisions of the appeals court are sent to the Supreme Court. There are eleven federal appeals courts. These are regional circuit courts that encompass several states. If the proposed amendment is ratified there should be six of the existing appeals courts in the new Red Country and five in the new Blue Country. The jurisdiction of some appeals courts will need to be adjusted so that they are totally in either the new Red Country or totally in the new Blue Country. After this adjustment each appeals court will be answerable to the new supreme court for the new country in which they reside. Only four of the eleven circuit courts of appeals will be affected. The eight states that will be affected are:

- Montana, Idaho, Arizona, and Alaska would be reassigned from the 9th Circuit Court of Appeals to the 10th Circuit Court of Appeals.
- Kentucky and Tennessee would be reassigned from the 6th Circuit Court of Appeals to the 10th Circuit Court of Appeals.
- west Virginia and Maryland would be reassigned from the 4th Circuit Court of Appeals to the 6th Circuit Court of Appeals as determined by the new Blue Country.

The current United States president, their cabinet, and the supreme court (reduced to three members) that exists just prior to the adoption of the amendment shall remain in office. They shall make no new laws or regulations after the amendment is adopted. Their most important duty will be to assure complete continuity in the transfer of the military and foreign affairs to the two new countries so that national security is not degraded. Their only other authorization will be the equitable distribution of all the federal assets and obligations including, but not limited to, the military, national debt, gold reserves, currency, monetary funds (pension, foreign accounts etc.), entitlements of Social Security and Medicare, etc. prior to the amendment to the two new sovereign states according to the 2010 population. The population split is about forty seven percent to the new Red Country and fifty three percent to the new Blue Country. The prescribed transfers should be performed in an orderly manner as expeditiously as possible.

Federal employees will actually not be greatly affected. Most are already located throughout the fifty states implementing federal services. In most cases these employees will continue the same day-to-day operations but report to either the Red Country federal government or the Blue Country federal government according to the state in which they live and provide services. Both the Blue Country and the Red Country will gradually change the duties of the federal government according to new and modified laws enacted by their respective congress and senate. Therefore, gradual changes will come, but there will also be time for equitable adjustments to employment responsibilities. The leaders of federal agencies in Washington D.C. will largely find new employment with one or the other new countries as their experiences and services will be in demand in each new country.

During the amendment implementation process, it will be necessary to continue the flow of federal funds from collection of federal income taxes, to borrowing money, and payment of federal obligations. The two new countries will need to quickly take charge of their separate federal tax collection and payment of obligations. I do not want to infer that I have a detailed plan for the flow of money during the transition. The plan needs to be drafted and executed independently by each of the two new countries. There will be many procedures that could be done together or in sequence to affect the desired rapid transfer of federal finances. I will, however, make three possible actions that could be taken to illustrate that this issue can and would be handled efficiently and that there would not be any interruption in income and expenses for both new federal governments and the people they serve. These three are:

- At the time the proposed amendment is ratified, the prior Treasury Department would be divided into two departments. One would handle the federal financial responsibility for the new Red Country and the other would handle the finances for the new Blue Country. The national debt would be split forty seven percent to the new Red Country and fifty three percent to the new Blue Country. New debt would be added to the account of the new country receiving the borrowed funds. All revenue from Income taxes, federal fees, etc., collected would be added to the new country account that has jurisdiction over the source of the income. All federal payments for Social Security, Medicare, Medicaid, military salary and needs, federal salaries, etc., would be made from the accounts set up for each new country. Then, in an organized sequence of events, the above operations would be transferred directly to the two new countries as fast as each new country can take charge of their finances.

- All states are currently collecting all sources of income (income taxes, fees, lotteries, services, etc.) from within their states. Each state could also efficiently collect all federal sources directly, and hold the funds in escrow for their new federal government until the new federal government can collect federal income. The states could make immediate payment of federal services until the new federal government can make the direct payments. With this plan, the old federal government (prior to the ratification of the proposed amendment) would directly apportion (by population) the national debt, all financial assets and liabilities and transfer these funds (and bills) direct to the two new countries. This way the two new federal governments would have control of their finances very expeditiously. Note that during the ratification period there will be a lot of time for planning so that there will be much preparation for the quick transfer of financial control.

- The old administration will be held over with custodial responsibilities as prescribed in the proposed amendment (chapter 4) Amendment Section IV. They could convert federal funding responsibility issue by issue. For example, the custodial federal government could totally disband the Department of Education, lay off all department personnel, and discontinue all federal regulations and mandates. They would then deposit, at each local school district, each student's share of the federal yearly budget for the school year. The 2012 department budget would be about $14 billion (source: http://ed.gov/about/overview/budget/statetables/12stbyprogram.pdf) and would be distributed to about fifty-five million students (source – www.census.gov/hhes/school/data/cps/2009/tables.html). This would be about $250 for each student. This would be appropriate since the Red Country would most likely not set up a department of education. Conversely, the new Blue Country would most likely establish a Department of Education that would have much more control over education than by the current Department of Education.

I could easily expound on a lot of details, but the transition will be clearly defined and there are literally millions of Americans that will be beneficially involved in establishing the new federal governments. Most of the specifics need to be left up to each new governing body to decide. This new activity will be in greater harmony with most individual's ideals, morals, needs, and expectations. Since the vast majority of Americans will support this amendment, its implementation will most likely be an easy, better, and more productive process than the present attempts to fix a broke and broken federal government. The following chapters discuss specific major issues as to what will be the further effect of the amendment.

Chapter 7

New National Boundaries & Populations

Let's first consider the effect of the proposed amendment on the new population alignment of the Blue Country and Red Country compared to other world countries. There should not be a concern with the population size of either of the two new countries. appendix E shows close to the current population of the fifteen most populated countries in the world. The current position of the United States is that we are the third most populated country in the world. appendix F shows the realignment of the world population after the current United States is replaced by the new Blue Country (to be ranked 6th in the world) and the new Red Country (to be ranked 9th just above Russia at number 10). Remember, the G8 will become the G9 with Americans having two votes instead of one! Now let's consider the new Blue Country and Red Country boundaries.

The new Red Country and Blue Country will basically have natural as well as political boundaries. The west common boundary is sparsely populated and extends from Canada on the north and Mexico on the south. The east boundary is basically the Northern section of the Mississippi River and the Ohio River. east of the Ohio River, the boundary should follow current state borders. Obviously the borders with Canada and Mexico will remain unchanged. See appendix A for the proposed map. This proposed definition of the new national boundaries provides for a reasonable and contiguous country for the new Red Country, except that Alaska will be separated from the lower states just as before the proposed amendment ratification. The new Blue Country has been defined as in appendix A so as to provide for the maximum majority of Blue thinking people. It should be obvious that the west coast in general, and California in particular, have politics, state governments, and citizens significantly more compatible with Northeast America than with the "fly over middle" and the Southern states. The Blue Country division of east coast and west coast is a small problem, discussed below, compared to the benefits. Blue thinking people will gain when separated from the overwhelmingly detrimental restraints that Red-thinking people place on the "progressive" agenda. This will make life better for all Blue thinking citizens.

It needs to be noted that the new Blue Country will have two land areas, basically east coast and west coast, separated by the new Red Country. Also of note is that the new Red Country will not have a west coast ocean port. There are mutual benefits that would minimize the effects of the portioned Blue Country and the Pacific Ocean restricted Red Country. NAFTA is currently in place, and will remain in place after the ratification of the proposed amendment. The only change NAFTA would experience would be expansion from the current three countries (Mexico, United States, and Canada) to four countries namely Canada, Mexico, Red Country and Blue Country. Therefore, there should be minimum interference (customs, security etc.) with goods and services being traded among the four countries. In addition, it would be advantageous to both new Countries to make additional accommodations. The Red Country could offer free trade, communications, and a transportation corridor from east to west to the Blue Country in exchange for a free trade, communications, and a transportation corridor to, and free use of, one or more west coast ports. There would be no need for any similar accommodations for the east coast since both the new Red Country and the New Blue Countries will both have equal access to the east coast.

The population of the two new countries, as determined by the 2010 census, is presented in appendix D. Note that the Washington D.C. population was included in the Blue Country numbers. I believe that there is a common consensus, as illustrated by their city politics, that Washington D.C. has a majority of Blue thinking people. It is particularly interesting to note that the two new countries will have almost equal populations. This in itself is very supportive of the proposition that it would be best for Americans that the current United States be divided according to the proposed amendment. Any objective statistical analysis will show that the proposed Red County and the proposed Blue Country are, in fact, two different populations in a very significant way. This country is actually divided politically because the citizens are truly socially and philosophically divided.

It must be considered that not all the people in the new Red Country will be receptive to a Red thought directed government. There will be many people who are very committed to Blue thought and direction. It would be just wrong to force anti-Blue laws on true Blue believers. It is similarly unjust for truly Red followers in the new Blue Country to be forced to comply with Blue laws they believe to be unconstitutional and unfair. The "power politics" of our federal government directed at imposing Blue principles on Red people, and vice versa, has led to a government that is broke and broken with less than twenty five percent of the people satisfied with Washington D.C.'s performance.

The proposed amendment provides for the majority of Red-thinking people to have a conservative Red thought-guided government, and equal provisions are made for the majority of Blue orientated people to have a progressive Blue style government; however, there will be many people that find they will be in the country that has values different from what they require. Strongly Blue thinking people will be very unhappy in the new Red Country, and vice versa. Section seven of the proposed amendment (chapter 4) gives all citizens a choice of which new country they wish to live in. For five years, every American will have dual citizenship so that they have equal rights in both the new Blue Country and the new Red Country. That will allow them to move into the country that best suits their beliefs before the five year dual citizenship period ends.

For example, a Red-thinking person in New York City (there might be a few) could wait and see the directions that the new Blue Country and the new Red Country follow. If everything is OK in the big apple (no harm, no foul), he or she can just continue pursuing the American dream as before the amendment was ratified. However, if that person finds the new Blue Country government is just unacceptable and the Red Country is much more desirable, they can relocate to the Red Country during the five year period. The amendment would guarantee through dual citizenship the right of each person to choose the government best for them for five years. After that time, each citizen will have single citizenship in their country of residence. Even then a person could apply for immigration approval to relocate from one country to the other just like a person today is free to apply for immigration to any country in the world.

Section seven of the proposed amendment has created more conversation with the people I have discussed the development of this book with than seemingly any other topic. Their first reaction was that there would be a vast migration of millions of Americans causing enormous disruption among the folks.

I have strongly opinionated friends of both the Red and Blue philosophies. Really, as difficult as that seems, I do. My Blue thinking friends think that millions of people would move to the new Blue Country because an unrestrained Blue progressive government is what almost everyone would want. My Blue friends believe that, given a choice, no one would move to the new Red Country that completely discounts social justice. They feel that this unrestrained population explosion in the new Blue Country would severely damage any chance the new Blue Country would have for a controlled implementation of progressive government. These friends, however, related to me that if the migration can be controlled, the amendment was a good idea, and it would be an ideal improvement in governance. Then the discussion would digress into the old rhetoric that America would progress to everyone's benefit if the federal government was permanently run by Blue committed people.

Guess what? My ardent friends who endorse Red-thinking believe just the opposite of my Blue thinking friends. "Texas could not handle half the population of California migrating within months after such a proposed amendment was ratified, and no one in their right mind would ever choose to move to California!" and similar phrases have been ardently proffered by my Red friends. These friends also told to me that if the migration can be controlled, the amendment was a good idea and would work ideally for an improvement in governance. Then the discussion would digress into the old rhetoric that America would progress to everyone's benefit if the federal government was permanently run by Red committed people.

So, keeping in mind the conversations with each group of Red and Blue friends, I don't believe that immigration would be a severe problem for both sides. In fact, I believe that we would find a balance of citizens that take advantage of emigrating from one country to another so that the net total number of immigrants for each country would be minimal. Generally, as a rule, people already live in a state which suits their values. This simple fact is reflected in their voting record. Of course, you have exceptions to every rule, but often they're minimal.

Let's focus upon voting record for a minute. A further discussion of the electorate analysis by the political parties and the demographics of the election process is presented in chapter 20. About fifty percent of qualified voters in America do not vote. They are called the "apathetic majority." It might be better to consider these citizens as not politically motivated. They are more concerned with their daily life, job, church, children, friends, health, income, and family. They are more concerned with meeting their financial needs than having any government involvement, including voting. As long as they can continue their daily lives peacefully and can meet their family and financial needs, they actually could care less about who is in charge of the government. By replacing the broke and broken current federal government with two new countries, everyone's life should get better. Both the new Red Country and the new Blue Country are based on sound principles of government. I truly believe that a government founded on proven principles and guided by like-minded motivated people will flourish. It is also true that every government does not need the same principles in order to succeed. Therefore, most of the citizens of America will be satisfied with their new country's government and will have little to no desire to migrate.

A quick review of appendices B and C will show that Republicans will have about seventy percent of the elected federal government in the new Red Country. Likewise, the Democrats will have about seventy percent of the elected new Blue Country federal government. Most Republicans lean Red and most Democrats lean Blue. It could easily be deduced that close to seventy percent of the voters will like their inclusion in either the new Red Country or the new Blue Country. Considering that only fifty percent of the people vote, it can be assumed that thirty-five percent of the population will like the politics of the new country in which they reside. Fifty percent of the apathetic people, and thirty-five percent of the voters, indicate that about eighty-five percent of the American population will actually prefer to be citizens of the new country in which they currently live.

Freedom to move from the Red Country to the Blue Country and vice versa does not mean it will be easy. Only the well motivated will actually pick up their families and move for political reasons. It will cost a lot of money to relocate and find new employment, so only the highly motivated will actually relocate. Assuming about eighty-five percent of the people will not want to move, there will be about fifteen percent that would consider moving for political reasons. Because of the cost and disruption to daily life, I think only a third (five percent of the population) of this group will actually move. That would represent about sixteen million Americans that might relocate. That would be about eight million people moving to the Blue Country, and about eight million people moving to the Red Country over a five year time span. We can do that; those aren't "large" numbers. At least citizens have a choice to get a more favorable government. This is a very small segment of the people with political concerns when one considers that about eighty percent (about 250 million people) of the population is dissatisfied with the present federal government.

There is another provision in section seven of the proposed amendment. A border state of the two new countries can petition to change from the Red Country to the Blue Country. This allows the people yet another chance to freely choose their style of government.

I believe that there are two states that may not fit the ideal goals of the proposed amendment. Colorado consists of a majority of Blue thinking people, but is an island in a sea of Red-thinking states. It is unrealistic to annex Colorado from the Red Country and give it to the new Blue Country. The second state I have a concern for is Indiana. It is a state that is as split politically as the nation. There is also the Constitution to consider.

The U.S. Constitution -Article IV - Section 3 - New States

"New States may be admitted by the Congress into this Union; but no new States shall be formed or erected within the Jurisdiction of any other State; nor any State be formed by the Junction of two or more States, or parts of States, without the Consent of the Legislatures of the States concerned as well as of the Congress."

Indiana is usually considered a Blue State in national politics. It is also considered a swing state that might vote Republican in a national election. Because of the slightly more Blue record, and given the proximity to strongly Blue states, Indiana has been proposed as a Blue Country state in the proposed amendment.

Indiana is a highly polarized state between Blue and Red-thinking residents. It might be better for all concerned if Indiana could divide itself during the ratification process after the amendment is adopted.

The Northern counties have a strong majority of Blue thinking people. These counties will be on the border of the proposed new Blue Country. The mid and Southern counties of Indiana are basically Red in their political thinking. These counties will be on the border of the proposed new Red Country. North of the Kankakee River from the state center to the west, and North of Route 6 from the state center to the east, has a very large majority of Blue thinking citizens and would be about two congressional districts. The rest of the state has a majority of Red-thinking citizens. If the northern counties were annexed to either Illinois and/or Michigan, those citizens would benefit and be part of the new Blue County. Then the remainder of Indiana (about seven congressional districts) would be included as part of the new Red Country. This accommodation would allow most Indiana citizens to be part of a new national government that is more compatible with the citizens.

According to the 2010 census, Indiana has a population of 6,501,582 people. If the Northern counties were annexed to Illinois and/or Michigan as suggested above, the new Indiana would have 5,193,974 people. Refer to appendix D. The figures for the Blue Country would be reduced by 5,193,974 people and the Red Country would be increased by the same number. With the Indiana adjustment the new Red Country would consist of forty-nine percent of the 2010 census count and the Blue Country would consist of fifty-one percent. Is that just a coincidence? Or, is that a validation that our country is actually split pretty much 50-50 Red and Blue, and the proposed amendment accommodates this 50-50 split along our divisive political and philosophical lines? Interesting, isn't it?

Part III

Transformation of America

Chapter 8

Social Security, Medicare and Medicaid

Social Security, Medicare, and Medicaid are among the most significant and perhaps the most important issues of the day. The reason it has one of the highest priorities today is that these promised entitlement benefits exceed the ability to cover the costs. Everyone agrees that the system will collapse if not reformed and the only argument is when it will collapse. The really good news is that all factions of the government want to reform the system so that it will adequately serve the next and future generations.

So what is the problem with a timely reform? The biggest problem is that our federal government is broke and broken so badly that it is dysfunctional when confronted with major national issues in general, and entitlements in particular. Once again we are faced with the ineffective elite Fifteen leaders in Washington as discussed in chapter 2. They are so polarized they simply cannot agree on anything but to increase the national debt. For Social Security, Medicare, and Medicaid reform they do nothing but "kick the can" down the road as if they expect it will be easier to fix the problem after it gets larger.

The elite Fifteen in Washington will control all efforts to make the necessary reforms to these entitlements. These elite people are very polarized. Each of the Fifteen is deeply committed to either Blue (generally progressive) or Red (generally conservative) ideology. This presents three possible options for effective reform. First, if the Fifteen are divided between Blue and Red ideology as we have seen since 2010, we see only inaction, otherwise known as gridlock, and nothing is done but demonizing rhetoric on both sides. Secondly, if the Fifteen are all in agreement with Red thought then it would be expected that there will be an extensive conservative based reform that will be forced on all Americans. This will alienate and motivate all progressive Blue thinking people so much that the reform will have little chance of success. The third alternative is that the Fifteen elite will all be committed to generally progressive Blue ideals. From 2009 through 2010, the elite Fifteen were all heavily committed to progressive Blue principles. However, they did not develop any reform to Social Security, Medicare, or Medicaid. They did expand coverage to more people thereby making the solvency of the programs in greater danger. Very few people have any confidence left that Washington D.C. will reform entitlements.

I contend that the best way to assure that these entitlements will be fully funded for the foreseeable future is that the proposed amendment be ratified as soon as possible. Then there would be two separate and different countries. One being predominantly Blue and one being predominately Red. The following might be some of the reform aspects that the Blue Country could be expected to adopt.

- The new Blue Country would extend coverage and include more participants. This would be paid for by redistribution of wealth through progressive taxation.
- Private retirement and health plans will be merged with Social Security, Medicare, and Medicaid to reduce the financing burden on the system.
- People with independent wealth or income would be excluded from these programs so that the truly needy can get the services they need.
- All qualified recipients would receive equal access to equal services.
- The total services available will be distributed equally among all recipients and that will guarantee the maximum services possible for everyone.
- The federal government could mandate states to fund federal programs.

The following might be some of the reform aspects that the Red Country could be expected to adopt

- Current Social Security, Medicare and Medicaid benefits will continue for current and soon to be eligible recipients.
- The enrollment age for Social Security and Medicare could be raised to seventy years of age so that there would be more funds available for the elderly. I'm seventy-one and, quite frankly, I do not need many age-related services.
- Younger citizens could be given a chance to invest in secure retirement programs in return for forgoing the entitlement programs thus reducing the financial burden on future Social security, Medicare, and Medicaid services.
- Services for the truly poor and dependant people would be enhanced and the services for the not so poor would be reduced so that the truly needy will receive adequate care.
- Business taxes might be reduced to produce an expanded economy so that there will be more funds for the entitlements. Also, through higher employment from a larger economy, less people will need entitlement services.
- All federal programs would need to be funded at the federal level. No federally unfunded mandates will be imposed upon states or local governments.

The proposed amendment is the only way for both Blue and Red-thinking people to do the things they truly believe will protect the entitlements. Both the Red thought and Blue thought factions deserve a chance to execute their programs. Both agree that without major action the entitlements will fail.

Both will do what they believe will benefit the system the best without being thwarted at every turn by opposing ideas.

Chapter 9

National Health Care

One of my first family discussion memories dates back to the late 1940s. At that time almost everyone basically paid for their own medical, hospital, and dentistry services. My father was worried that someday he might not have enough savings to pay for unexpected medical expenses. This subject was important since I just had my tonsils removed, my grandmother had a hospital stay, and my mother had a hysterectomy. Mom and Dad were considering some new form of health insurance. This was Blue Cross to cover hospital costs (with a deductable) and the other was Blue Shield (with a deductible) for doctor fees. Of particular concern were the choices for hospital care. There were three choices for a private room: semiprivate, a two-patient shared room, or a four patient ward. The choice was up to my parents and they had to balance risks and services with their ability to pay for the services. The family was responsible for their own health care after all. My parents chose to pay a premium to cover a semiprivate room for all days over the allowed two days per sickness. They also chose a $500 deductable for doctor and surgeon services. The insurance company had very little to say about which hospital or doctors the family decided to use. My parents decided on the amount and level of care, and were ultimately responsible for payment

Over the last fifty years, this family responsibility gradually shifted to an insurance company responsibility. The insurance coverage lead to what was termed as a "third party payee." The process involved the patients, hospitals, and doctors in determining the services desired and the payment responsibility shifted from the patient to the insurance company. Consequently, the cost of the demanded services rose disproportionately to the financial capability of the patients. In order to cover the resultant increase in premiums, the cost of the insurance was shifted to employers because individuals could not pay for the services they demanded. Not surprisingly, the cost of health care rose at a much higher rate than personal income. Currently, a great many employees expect their employers to provide the best health care available. Everyone demands a private room, and the semi-private rooms (much less four room wards) have all but disappeared.

Also in the equation were the public sector employees who demanded that their health care services had to be equal to, or better than, in the private sector. Another dramatic health care cost escalator for society was the unemployed, elderly, and poor who demand equal (and free) health care service. Thus, health care costs have escalated exponentially compared to individual's incomes.

As an example of the current disconnect between the patient and health care costs can be seen in the education system. I chose this example since my wife is a retired teacher and one of my sons is a young certified teacher. Their health insurance exceeds $11,000 per year paid by the taxpayer as are their salaries. They are denied the choice of receiving $11,000 pretax income per year to their salaries in exchange for cancelling their current insurance coverage and purchasing alternate health insurance. This example is not unique in today's society.

Today, the health care provided in America is the best in the world in spite of all these cost and service problems. The down side is that health care is so costly today that there is no commonly accepted way to pay for it. Most Americans today demand that their individual health care must be the best available, and many also believe that the government should guarantee payment of health services. This is compounded because future costs will far surpass current costs. Almost everyone believes, and rightly so, that significant reform is needed in order to retain the best health care system in the world.

Both Blue and Red-thinking people agree that the health care system needs significant reform. However, here again Blue thinking people and Red-thinking people have diametrically opposed ideas for reform. From 2009 through 2010, all of the elite Fifteen in control of the federal government were committed to Blue thought. Consequently, a comprehensive reform of health care was enacted into national law that was entirely based on Blue beliefs which will be forced on all Americans including all Red-thinking people.

Never in the last 100 years has one single piece of legislation caused such divisiveness in this country. Never in the last 100 years has any single piece of legislation expanded the federal government as much as Obama Care. Never in this country has the federal government, through legislation, taken control over every citizen's personal health care. This legislation truly has fundamentally changed the federal government like none other.

Let me make my position perfectly clear. I am not condemning Obama Care itself. I truly believe that it has significant merit for Blue thinking people. I also believe that Red-thinking people are just as compassionate and concerned with everyone's health, but the Red-thinking people have significantly different ideas as to how best to provide good health care for everyone. I firmly believe that the ratification of the proposed amendment is the best and workable way to satisfy the vast majority of Americans. After ratification, the new Blue Country (see appendix A) would simply continue with the implementation of Obama Care making minor adjustments as time goes by. In contrast, the new Red Country would repeal the entire Obama Care legislation on day one and start developing an intensive health care program geared to predominately Red thought. This action for the future of health care will be considerably desired by most Americans.

I will not try to comment on the content and effect of this legislation, nor will I try to make a case that Obama Care is good, bad, or indifferent. That would take volumes and the country would still be strongly divided as to the benefits and problems with implementing Obama Care. I am only trying to relate this legislation to the increasing problems with Washington D.C. and how the proposed amendment would affect this, and future, legislation.

Please recall chapter 2 and my discussion on the makeup and power of the elite Fifteen in Washington D.C. In my opinion, the concentrated power garnered by the elite Fifteen is the prime reason for the present "Broke and Broken" condition of Washington D.C. that threatens the very future of the United States. In 2008, the election of the president, congress, and senate produced an elite consisting of fifteen people who were all dedicated to Blue thinking. Obama Care is an example of the power of the elite Fifteen and the direction the Fifteen will take when given a chance. Remember how Obama Care was created? Behind closed doors. The elite Fifteen drafted the most extensive change American life ever written. It was totally compliant with the Blue thinking and there were no attempts to consider Red-thinking citizens' desires or expectations. The elite Fifteen knew that a significant voting majority of congress and the senate were Democrats.

As explained in chapter 2, the Fifteen had supreme control from all the legislative priorities down to individual office staffs for all Democrat members. It took only several months of arm twisting and special side deals with some Red leaning Democrats to get a lock step voting majority for the legislation. Then, on a dark and stormy night, Obama Care was passed through congress and the senate with lock step Democrat votes, and no open debate as to the actual contents of the legislation. The best summary of the overwhelming control exercised by the elite Fifteen over Obama Care was from one of the elite, Speaker of the House, Nancy Pelosi. She said, "We have to pass this bill to find out what is in it." None of the representatives or senators had time to review, study, or comment on the contents of the legislation. This legislation proved to the elite Fifteen that as long as they were totally Blue thinking leaders, they could do anything they wanted to. The congress and senate members were irrelevant. The Fifteen also celebrated the fact that they had not only the power to make totally Blue legislation, but they could also force compliance by the nearly half of the country who preferred Red-thinking in their government. This demonstrated power to force just under half the people to conform to an offensive (in their minds) political philosophy is why this country is so irreconcilably and deeply divided.

Please do not believe that the above diatribe was a condemnation of Obama Care. My point is that the process that instituted the legislation is wrong. It is just unfair to half the country when they must accept unwanted law. Also, it needs to be acknowledged that if the elite Fifteen were all of Red thought they would pass great and sweeping laws that conform to Red philosophy and would force the Blue people to conform to heinous (in their minds) laws. That would be equally unfair to nearly half of the people. When the Fifteen are mixed with both Red and Blue committed members you get what was typical for 2011: A fully nonfunctioning federal government that just gets bigger as each side tries to buy votes with federal funds in order to get complete Red or Blue control of the elite Fifteen membership. There are no indications that the federal government will change from within, and it has too much power to be changed from outside. Consider this: The adoption and ratification of the proposed amendment would bypass an already broke and broken Washington D.C. The states have the power as provided for in the Constitution to draft and ratify an amendment. This would let Red-thinking people do what Red people believe what is right to do without restraints from Blue thinking people, and vice versa. A policy of "live and let live" is not all bad.

Red-thinking people, who number in the tens of millions, are full of fury and scorn over the imposition of Obama Care. This is major national discontent. This growing discontent is further dividing this country and inserts the added feelings of anger and basic freedoms lost. The Blue responses are statements that basically say to just "get over it" because it is the constitutional law of the land. And the lines in the sand get deeper.

In January 2011, the Republicans took control of the House of Representatives from the Democrats. Expressing the deep concerns for Red-thinking people, they passed legislation to repeal Obama Care by a vote of 242 Republicans and 3 Democrats for the repeal. 189 Democrats opposed to the repeal. The House legislation was passed on January 19, 2011 just nineteen days after Red Congressional control was established. The Senate, which was controlled by the Democrat leadership, knew that the Senate was lock step divided on party lines. On February 2nd 2011, they allowed a vote on the repeal which recorded 51 senators against the repeal of Obama Care (all Democrats) and 47 (all Republicans) in favor of a repeal. This exercise was obviously devoid of any negotiations, solved nothing, and further divided and polarized the federal government in the country.

The argument goes on. Now it is clear just how polarizing and divisive Obama Care is. Within two months, fourteen states filed suit in federal court that Obama Care was unconstitutional, followed by thirteen additional states by January 12, 2001. When twenty-seven states, more than half the country, sue the federal government on the same issue there is a major governance problem in America. The following are the twenty-seven states filing suits to repeal Obama care are:

Suing State	Suit Filed		Notes
Virginia	March 23, 2010		1.) * indicates Blue Country (8 total)
Florida	March 23, 2010		2.) 27 states have active suits to
South	March 23, 2010		repeal Obama Care
Nebraska	March 23, 2010		3.) Only 34 states are needed to call
Texas	March 23, 2010		a Constitutional Convention
Utah	March 23, 2010		
Louisiana	March 23, 2010		
Alabama	March 23, 2010		
Michigan	March 23, 2010	*	
Colorado	March 23, 2010		
Pennsylvania	March 23, 2010	*	
Washington	March 23, 2010	*	
Idaho	March 23, 2010		
South Dakota	March 23, 2010		
North Dakota	April 5, 2010		
Arizona	April 6, 2010		
Georgia	April 13, 2010		
Alaska	April 20, 2010		
Nevada	May 14, 2010	*	
Indiana	May 14, 2010	*	
Mississippi	May 14, 2010		
Wisconsin	January 3, 2011	*	
Oklahoma	January 7, 2011		
Wyoming	January 7, 2011		
Ohio	January	*	
Kansas	January		
Maine	January	*	

It is interesting to note that eight of the twenty-seven states vehemently opposed to Obama care will be from the Blue Country if the proposed amendment is ratified. One common comment from these eight states is that they simply cannot afford to pay for the implementation of Obama Care. Another observation is that most of these eight states are generally considered "swing states" during an election cycle. This means that even though they are basically Blue in philosophy, there is a significant portion of the people that prefer laws in favor of Red beliefs.

In these swing states, the national Blue leadership will concentrate on creating candidates that are attractive to Red-thinking people, but are not truly Red-thinking people. The purpose of this strategy is for majority control at the national level for Blue elected officials. The Blue leadership will be careful not to motivate the Red-thinking people within these swing states to vote in large numbers and threaten their already Blue national majority. Conversely, the Red national leadership has the same strategy and motivation in swing states to protect their national majority.

This highly polarized issue in America is far from being resolved. The current suits by the above states can only be addressed and decided by the supreme court. This is an absolutely futile waste of time. The supreme court decision will only further polarize the country. It has too long been an advocate for and against popular political issues and has long lost its acknowledged credentials for interpreting laws according to the constitution. The ultimate decision of the supreme court will settle nothing. If Obama Care is ruled constitutional, the Blue thinking people across the country will be very happy and the Red-thinking people will be more wrathful than a "woman scorned." If the supreme court finds Obama Care unconstitutional, the Red-thinking people will be very happy, but beware the backlash from all those that demand Obama Care. Does anyone think that the supreme court will change anyone's deeply held convictions for or against Obama Care?

Once again let me make my position perfectly clear. I am not condemning Obama Care itself. I truly believe that it has significant merit for Blue thinking people. I also believe that Red-thinking people are just as compassionate and concerned with everyone's health, but the Red-thinking people have significantly different ideas as to how best to provide good health care for everyone. I firmly believe that the ratification of the proposed amendment is the best and workable way to satisfy the vast majority of Americans. After ratification, the new Blue Country (see appendix A) would simply continue with the implementation of Obama Care making minor adjustments as time goes by. In contrast, the new Red Country would repeal the entire Obama Care legislation on day one and start developing an intensive health care program geared to predominately Red thought. This action for the future of health care will be considerably desired by most Americans.

Obama Care, as discussed above, is a prime example of what happens when the elite Fifteen are all disciples of Blue thought. Be very assured that if the Fifteen elite leaders become all disciples of Red thought, new legislation will emerge that will be as large as Obama Care and equally despised and rejected by the powerless Blue thinking portion of the public. For the last thirty years, we have seen the results when the elite Fifteen are a mix of dedicated Red and Blue committed leaders. We have seen ever increasing bickering in Washington D.C. Special interest groups will still get special ear marks and parochial loopholes in an attempt by both forces to gain a majority power. Washington D.C. will continue to grow as more promises are made to attain and hold power. Forget balanced federal budgets and fiscal restraint. In the divided arena pitting Red against Blue, success will come to those who promise the most, regardless of the debt or unintended consequences involved.

Ratification of the proposed amendment creating two separate and sovereign countries will allow the irreversibly divided United States to evolve into 1.) A unified country with Blue thinking people pursuing the lives they desire and 2.) A unified country with Red-thinking people pursuing the lives they desire. The amendment is a peaceful solution for a polarized country with a problem that is perceived unsolvable. "Blessed are the peacemakers, for they will be called the sons of God" The Bible, Matthew 5:9

Chapter 10

Immigration

"But the real problem is not immigration but assimilation. Anyone can do immigration. But if you don't assimilate the immigrants ... then immigration becomes not an asset but a liability"
 . The Washington Post - Charles Krauthammer, June 17, 2005

"We cannot welcome those to come and then try and act as though any culture will not be respected or treated inferior. We cannot look at the Latino community and preach 'one language.'"
- Al Sharpton

When I was in grade school our family farm produced, among other things, strawberries. The season was fairly short and in late spring we all participated in picking strawberries for market. Frequently, some of my brother's teenage friends and I would help pick berries for $0.10 a quart and each friend would only pick as many as they wanted to earn the extra cash. Note that this wholesome activity is now frowned upon as abusive child labor. Back then it was a voluntary developmental source for minors to learn how to earn money and develop cash management. As the season developed there were more berries to be picked than could be picked by my family and friends. My father would go to Glassboro to a "labor camp" (now it would be called a migrant worker dormitory) and ask for volunteers to pick berries and earn $0.10 a quart. Out of the many workers there, my father always found experienced and willing berry pickers. These workers were primarily from Puerto Rico. They would arrive from their homes in Puerto Rico in the early spring and work through early fall harvesting crops for the wide variety of produce grown in our part of Southern New Jersey. After the season was over, they would take their earnings back home to help support their families.

I had many discussions with these migrant workers while picking berries. Most only spoke rudimentary English, but all were eager to practice and learn more English speaking skills. I enjoyed these conversations and found that the workers I worked with were all very nice, polite, and hard working. Many were very happy to live with their families in Puerto Rico in the winter and support them with their American summer earnings. Several wished to immigrate to the United States. They all knew the process of getting a permanent work permit, having an extended visa, and applying for U.S. citizenship. They all knew they had to learn basic English speaking skills so that they could understand legal documents, newspapers, and normal everyday conversational English. They all also knew that they had to apply for, study for, earned citizenship. This was a lengthy process but those who wanted to immigrate eagerly took up the challenge. I grew up understanding a guest worker program and a path to citizenship that worked and was fair to workers and immigrants alike. My, my, my how times have changed!

Immigration and its control is second only to the Obama Care issue as the most divisive and polarizing factor affecting the progress of America. For the last thirty years, America's immigration policy and control has continuously deteriorated. The continuation of unresponsive corrective actions, and the ever increasing national polarization over immigration, is proof that this issue will not be solved without severe dissatisfaction for most Americans.

Despite these potential disagreements, areas of agreement do exist between Blue and Red-thinking people over the issue of immigration. Both acknowledge that immigration has been a valuable asset for generations and should be encouraged in the future. Immigrants have helped build America into the greatest country in the world. Both agree that immigrants have, for generations, positively added to our labor force and the productivity of America. Both agree that America will benefit significantly with a continued inflow of immigrants. Both agree that America is a 'people-magnet' and that immigrants to America will continue to far outnumber the Americans that emigrate from America to other nations. Finally, both agree that the national immigration policy has been a failure for more than twenty years and that extensive reform is needed now. Further delays will just exacerbate the failed policy.

With so much agreement, why is there so much discord? Simply put: it's political. There is complete disagreement between Red and Blue philosophy as to how future immigration should be promoted and controlled. Highlights of the differences as I see them are:

Red ideas for a good immigration policy:

- Secure the borders and stop undocumented immigration.
- Enforce existing immigration laws and promote legal immigration.
- Institute a "guest worker" program that would allow for foreign nationals to enter the country for purposes of gainful employment.
- Deport undocumented immigrants that do not obey national and state laws.
- Deny citizenship to babies born in America when neither parent is an American Citizen.
- Provide a path to citizenship for prior undocumented immigrants and require new immigrants to apply for citizenship according to current laws in order to gain citizenship.
- Only grant citizenship to immigrants that commit to assimilate into American culture.
- Establish English as the official national language.

Blue ideas for a good immigration policy

- Acknowledge that the borders cannot be sealed and recognize that undocumented immigrants will always be a factor. Promote "open borders" as a policy.
- Revise current immigration laws so that undocumented immigrants are not deported if they want to stay in the country.
- Make employers solely responsible for establishing citizenship for employment.
- Recognize that all residents of America (citizens, foreign nationals and undocumented immigrants alike) will have equal access to government services that are loosely characterized as "entitlements."
- Provide "safe havens" for undocumented residents even if they violate state and federal laws. Law violators are entitled to the same legal guarantees afforded to citizens.
- Encourage preservation of foreign cultures in immigrant-dominant areas and discourage any changes needed to assimilate into the traditional American culture.
- Provide a reasonable path to citizenship for any resident that is not a citizen.
- Recognize all foreign languages of immigrants for all public discourse.

Even if the above is overstated or understated, the general consensus of most Americans is that the political division in the approach to immigration control is hopelessly divided. As long as the elite Fifteen in Washington D.C. are divided between Red and Blue committed people (chapter 2), workable immigration reform will not be developed. If the Fifteen elite remain Blue for several years, their Blue ideas will be the adopted national immigration policy and the Red-thinking Americans will be forced to obey. The opposite is equally true if the elite Fifteen in Washington are all elected Red thinkers and remain in office for several years. It is this threat of force by one half of the nation over the other half, or the continued inaction for a comprehensive immigration policy, that makes this political divide such a large polarizing issue today second only to Obama Care.

Voter base is another factor that enters the discussion of immigration. The dominant issue concerning immigration largely involves multigenerational undocumented immigrants from our good neighbor, Mexico. Red-thinking politicians are attempting to show how a documented law abiding immigration policy will be the best way to assimilate immigrants into American culture. Blue thinking politicians are also attempting to garner votes by assuring all immigrants, both documented and undocumented, equal social justice as enjoyed by American citizens. This is an increasingly expanding effort by both factions as they both believe that there are sufficient votes to sway the control of the elite Fifteen as totally Red or totally Blue committed. Both sides promise their positions will be implemented if they gain complete political control. As stated many times in this book: this strategy of using force to implement Blue policy over Red committed people, and vice versa, is the main cause for the broke and broken condition in Washington D.C.

Immigration policy is now so divided that Red leaning states are passing laws independently from federal administration to reform immigration policy as necessary to protect themselves from an out-of-control immigration policy. The Blue committed federal administration is now legally trying to stop states from any attempt to institute any Red leaning reforms. And the political division intensifies.

Published comments for some of the new state laws are presented below. All the new state immigration reform laws are being sued by the administration in Washington.

Alabama – Source: http://www.bloomberg.com/news/2011-08-01/alabama-immigration-law-imporperly-encroaches-on-federal-power-u-s-says.html

"Alabama Governor Robert Bentley signed the law broadening police powers on June 9, following Arizona Governor Jan Brewer in requiring local authorities to identify illegal immigrants. The law is set to take effect on Sept. 1.
The measure requires police officers to verify the immigration status of anyone they stop and suspect may be in the U.S. illegally. Businesses must use a federal database called E- Verify to determine whether job applicants are eligible to work. In addition, the law makes it a crime to rent housing to illegal immigrants. Alabama is the fifth U.S. state to enact such legislation."

Arizona – Source:

http://topics.nytimes.com/top/reference/timestopics/subjects/i/immigration-and-emigration/arizona-immigration-law-sb-1070/index.html

"The legislation requires police officers, "when practicable," to detain people they reasonably suspect are in the country without authorization and to verify their status with federal officials, unless doing so would hinder an investigation or emergency medical treatment. The law also makes it a state crime — a misdemeanor — to not carry immigration papers. In addition, it allows people to sue local government or agencies if they believe federal or state immigration law is not being enforced."

Additional Source – http://nation.foxnews.com/arizona-immigration-law/2011/05/26/us-supreme-court-upholds-ariz-business-immigration-law

"The supreme court has sustained Arizona's law that penalizes businesses for hiring workers who are in the United States illegally, rejecting arguments that states have no role in immigration matters.
By a 5-3 vote, the court said Thursday that federal immigration law gives states the authority to impose sanctions on employers who hire unauthorized workers.
The decision upholding the validity of the 2007 law comes as the state is appealing a ruling that blocked key components of a second, more controversial Arizona immigration enforcement law.

Thursday's decision applies only to business licenses and does not signal how the high court might rule if the other law comes before it.

Chief Justice John Roberts, writing for a majority made up of Republican-appointed justices, said the Arizona's employer sanctions law "falls well within the confines of the authority Congress chose to leave to the states." Justices Stephen Breyer, Ruth Bader Ginsburg and Sonia Sotomayor, all Democratic appointees, dissented. The fourth Democratic appointee, Justice Elena Kagan, did not participate in the case because she worked on it while serving as President Barack Obama's solicitor general."

Florida – Source: http://www.nytimes.com/2011/05/05/us/05florida.html

"The bill would require the police to make "a reasonable effort" to determine the immigration status of people they arrest and jail, a provision that opponents say is an Arizona-style attack on legal and illegal immigrants. The proposal would also require that illegal immigrants who are convicted of nonviolent crimes be referred to federal officials for deportation."

Georgia – Source - http://www.nytimes.com/2011/05/14/us/14georgia.html

"One of the Georgia law's authors, Matthew L. Ramsey, a Republican state legislator, said the measure was written to withstand legal challenges. Lawmakers set clear guidelines on when the police are allowed to request a suspect's immigration status, he said. The law allows state and local police officers to request immigration documentation from criminal suspects and, if they do not receive it, to take the suspects to jails, where federal officials could begin the deportation process.

"States don't have the legal authority to deport. We don't have the legal authority to secure our borders," Mr. Ramsey said. "But our goal is, within a constitutional framework, to eliminate incentives for illegal aliens to cross into our state."

The law also creates stricter requirements for businesses hiring workers and harsher punishments for anyone who harbors or employs an illegal immigrant. There are 425,000 illegal immigrants in Georgia, the seventh most of any state, the Pew Hispanic Center estimates. Two other Southern states, Alabama and South Carolina, are also considering similar immigration bills that are expected by many experts to pass this year."

Nebraska – Source - http://www.theawl.com/2011/04/six-degrees-north-of-arizona-nebraskas-war-on-immigration

"Nebraska is starting to look a lot like Arizona—legally, at least. Over the past few years, the state has enacted a spate of anti-immigration laws; and whether it's State Senator Charlie Janssen's unconstitutional witch hunt against all brown people, an ordinance in Fremont that bars employers from hiring illegal immigrants and landlords from renting to them, or, the latest assault, a law that denies public assistance to legal immigrants who have lived in the country less than five years, it seems the legislature and governor have one thing on their minds: making Nebraska a less friendly, less tolerant state. In February, Governor Dave Heineman ordered the legislature to strip undocumented workers of pre-natal care, a move that drew sharp condemnation even from traditional Republican allies like Nebraska Right to Life."

Utah – Source http://www.usatoday.com/news/nation/2011-03-08-utah08_ST_N.htm

"The Utah Legislature passed a pair of immigration bills aimed at striking a balance between people who want to deport all illegal immigrants and those who want to integrate them into American society.

The other bill passed late Friday would allow the state to grant work permits to illegal immigrants who undergo a criminal background check, pay fines of up to $2,500 and learn English. The bill would require Gov. Gary Herbert, a Republican, to seek a federal waiver, since immigration law makes it a crime to knowingly hire illegal immigrants."

In addition to the states above with adopted new immigration laws, Texas is an example of the momentum for several other states attempting to take control of Immigration.

"More than 100 immigration-related bills are pending in the Texas legislature alone, including those that would give state and local police officers the authority to enforce federal immigration laws, make English the official language, and prevent undocumented students from getting in-state tuition and scholarships." Source: http://abcnews.go.com/Politics/immigration-wars-texas-georgia-oklahoma-arizona-style-laws/story?id=13050716

There is another very important issue to remember here. For Blue leaning Obama Care, there are twenty-seven Red leaning states suing the federal government to repeal the legislation, and all the states that pass immigration reform are being sued by the Blue leaning federal administration. There are at least twenty-seven states that have passed, or are in the process of passing, Red-leaning immigration legislation. The fact that there are states suing the federal government, and the federal government suing the states on the two largest issues of the day, speaks volumes. When two entities that are supposed to be "married" in governance are suing each other, it's time for a divorce decree, don't you think?

Adoption of the proposed amendment would create such a divorce that would let each party go their separate ways and be free to prosper as each individual wishes. Again, as I have stated several times before, "live and let live" is not all bad. What might happen if the proposed amendment was ratified?

Based on recent news commentaries, it is reasonable that if the Red Country was an independent country, the Southern border would be "sealed" and a new immigration policy based on most if not all the "Red ideas for a good immigration policy" listed above in this chapter. It is also true that if the Blue Country was an independent country, there would be open borders and their version of an ongoing immigration policy based on social justice for all residents as the "Blue ideas for a good immigration policy" listed above. Thus, both new countries can carry out their commitments to their constituents without interference from another country. I truly believe that both sides would agree that peaceful solutions to national problems avoid hostility, frustration, and potential violence.

Chapter 11

Division of Federal Property

The division of Federal property from the current United States to the two new countries is extremely important, but can be covered in a very short chapter.

All federal property outside Washington D.C. should be assumed by the new country in which the property is located as soon as the proposed amendment is ratified. This includes all federal lands, facilities, equipment, resource rights, and all other non-military federal property. (The military is discussed in Chapter 12). It should be recognized that the federal offices outside Washington D.C. are reasonably spread out according to the states' needs and apportioned to people served. For example, the federal offices in Denver will remain, and be staffed by, the same personnel and will perform federal services exactly as before the amendment is adopted. The only exception would be that they are now under the administration of the new Red Country. Just as before the ratification, these federal employees will adjust their activities and will be directed by the new country's congress and administration. They will subsequently be federal employees of the new country.

It stands to reason that Washington D.C. would become the capitol of the new Blue Country because so many government facilities are already in place for a federal government. The new Red Country will need to designate a location for its capitol as per their constitution. The federal properties in the surrounding areas around Washington D.C. revert to the states of Maryland and Virginia as they are presently located. For example, the Pentagon and C.I.A. facilities are in Virginia, a state in the new Red Country. The extensive government service facilities in Maryland will be part of the new Blue Country.

It would be an interesting subject to consider that some areas in and around Washington D.C. be established as a monument to the heritage common to both new countries. These areas, like the National Mall and the Arlington Cemetery, could be set up to be freely used and maintained by both new countries.

The only troublesome federal property division will be for the foreign embassies. There are several embassy locations in developed nations. An equitable division for both new countries to be represented in secure facilities can be jointly negotiated between the two new countries and the host country. For the countries with only one embassy facility, there would either need to be shared accommodations, or one of the new countries would need to construct a new embassy. This will be difficult, but solvable.

Chapter 12

Military Realignment

The most important function for any sovereign government is the defense of the country. The United States has the best equipped, trained, and deployed national defense system in the world. As the world's only superpower, our military is arguably more than twice as effective as any other military system of any other country in the world. It is my true belief that the current United States armed services can be effectively divided with complete continuity of the military mission, and the preservation of national security. It is also reasonable to expect that each of the new military systems will excel over any other world power. I also believe that if we do not adopt the proposed amendment, our nation's military and national security will continue to be degraded as it becomes more difficult to currently fund our military. Remember, we are currently a divided country with a broke and broken government (chapters 1 and 2). Given this fact, along with an ever increasing national debt, it is clear that our military will be severely degraded in the near and foreseeable future. It will be to the benefit of all Americans to have the two most powerful military systems that can be maintained, instead of a single deteriorating military. The proposed amendment to divide the United States into the Red Country and the Blue country provides the best path to assure that our national security will continue to be the world's best for generations to come.

There are many branches of the military that all must be evaluated with regard to the effect of the ratification of the proposed amendment. These are the Coast Guard, National Guard, Army, Navy, Air Force, Marines, and the massive supply chain supporting these forces. The related security provided by the F.B.I., C.I.A., and Homeland Security agencies will be discussed at the end of this chapter.

U.S. Coast Guard

"The U.S. Coast Guard is authorized to enforce, or assist in the enforcement of, all U.S. Federal laws applicable on, over, and under the high seas and waters subject to the jurisdiction of the United States. These include laws which provide for the U.S. Coast Guard to exclusively act, and those which the Coast Guard enforces primarily for some other Federal agency. Generally, the Coast Guard must determine on a case-by-case basis whether it has jurisdiction. Along with that, it often must also determine whether an assertion of jurisdiction is consistent with international law. In many cases involving a foreign vessel, the Coast Guard decides whether it has jurisdiction over the vessel and its personnel based on three elements: the activities of the vessel and personnel, the location of the vessel, and the nationality of the vessel."

Source:

www.uscg.mil/INTERNATIONAL/affairs/Publications/MMSCode/english/Chap3. htm

"Altogether, this small service with a very big job numbers only about 87,000 personnel. By comparison, the next smallest U.S. armed force is the Marine Corps with over 198,000 active duty members alone." Source: http://uscg.mil/doctrine/CGPub/Pub_1.pdf

The U.S. Coast Guard is divided into nine districts that cover the fifty states. Each district is autonomously set up with national oversight. These districts are basically established along the same lines as the two new countries created by the proposed amendment. In order to completely separate the U.S. Coast Guard, each district should be totally encompassed in either the Blue Country or the Red Country. To accomplish this division, eleven states (only two coastal) need to be reassigned from one current district to another. The mountain states, which have very little U.S. Coast Guard presence, Montana,

Idaho, Utah, and Arizona, should be reassigned to District 8 based in New Orleans. Next, Minnesota would be reassigned to the District 8. The inland states of Illinois, Indiana, Ohio, and west Virginia would be reassigned to Great Lakes District 9. The only two coastal states affected would be Virginia and North Carolina, who should be reassigned to District 7 headquartered in Florida. All other states would see no changes at the district level.

The equipment and facilities ownership would be simply transferred from the old United States to the new country in which it is located. Also, consider that almost all of the personnel and their families live relatively close to their assigned bases, so relocation of personnel will be limited. The current national U.S. Coast Guard administration would be divided and about half assigned to provide national continuity to the new Red Country and about half to the new Blue Country. Lastly, it should be realized that the current missions and activities would not be changed as all U.S. Coast Guard activity emanates from the closest base involved.

The general public would see no change is the operation and performance of the U.S. Coast Guard after the proposed amendment is ratified. Most importantly, there would be no disruption of the Coast Guard-provided security associated with the ratification of the proposed amendment. Even the supply chain for the Coast Guard will not be affected by the ratification of the proposed amendment. Most supply resources are local in proximity to the bases. Purchases of these resources, as well as necessary equipment, will still be made from open competitive private businesses both domestic and foreign. The greatest advantage gained from the ratification of the proposed amendment would be to the personnel and their families. As for the rest of the country, most of the Coast Guard personnel are either Blue or Red-thinking citizens, and the proposed amendment ratification would provide most personnel and their families with a federal government that is consistent with their ideals and expectations of federal government performance.

National Guard

The National Guard is considered by most Americans as a major force for state security and help in state emergencies. In this book I consider the Air National Guard and the Army National Guard to be the same entity, referred to simply as the National Guard. Generally speaking, the National Guard is more responsive to citizen's daily needs than the major branches of the National military. Today, the National Guard has an additional huge added value: It has many battle-tested personnel in foreign military engagements because of its important role in Iraq, Afghanistan, and other foreign military operations. Even though those are coordinated national activities, the National Guard has always been, and still is, totally answerable to state governments. Each state has control of its National Guard. The current National Guard system is completely compatible with the proposed amendment. Keep in mind the division of the country will be defined along state boundaries. Therefore, for the National Guard in each of those states will experience no change in the personnel, facilities, equipment, administration, or daily activities during the entire process of amendment formation, ratification, and implementation. Even the supply chain for the National Guard will not be affected by the ratification of the proposed amendment. Most supply resources are local in proximity to the bases. Purchases of these resources, as well as necessary equipment, will still be made from open competitive private businesses both domestic and foreign.

It should be comforting to all the citizens that the ratification and implementation of the proposed amendment will be supported by the ongoing broad-based security provided by the National Guard. The major change to each of the National Guards during and following the ratification of the proposed amendment will be that there will be a change in their relationship with their federal government. The National Guards are state organizations and the proposed amendment will ensure each and every National Guard with a federal government that is much more compatible with their basic beliefs and expectations. For example, National Guards in Red Country will have a federal government that has a controlling majority of Red-thinking elected officials. The same advantage will be granted to Blue National Guards within the new Blue Country. No longer will National Guard personnel from Red states be forced by a Blue controlled federal government to participate in foreign military conflicts pursuing Blue thought goals, and vice versa. However, if there is a common enemy to both the new Blue Country and the new Red country, there will be mutual cooperation among the fifty state national guards because the cause will be mutually important.

Army, Navy, Air Force, and Marines

First of all, let me make a cogent statement of the most important fact. We are not at war with ourselves. The ratification of the proposed amendment is a peaceful process that actually reduces internal hostility between Red and Blue thinking people that have so divided this great nation. The proposed amendment is not, in any way, to be confused with a secession movement. A succession movement would be a forced separation of the nation which infers forceful hostility, whereas the amendment process is a constitutionally authorized, peaceful, and methodical action that benefits our two divided philosophies as discussed in chapter 1.

The proposed amendment would keep all current military obligations in place for both the new Red Country and the new Blue Country. The only assumed addition would be an all-inclusive mutual defense agreement between the two new countries. Both would be members of the United

Nations, NATO, and all other current foreign organizations where the United States is currently a member. At the time the proposed amendment is ratified, the world should understand that the two new countries will initially speak as one. This would continue until the new countries duly change their treaties regarding world issues just as any other independent sovereign country would do. We should all expect that if during the amendment process we should be faced with a foreign attack, or a third world war, the two new countries would stand and defend each other as one unified people under the current United States paradigm. The proposed amendment can be implemented with no lapse in our mutual national defense.

Afghanistan offers a good military example regarding both the simplicity and complexity for the origination of two new countries replacing the old United States. The war effort is currently a coalition of several nations. After the amendment is adopted there would just be a change in our country's names only, and both the new Blue Country and the new Red Country would be fully supportive members of the coalition independently from each other; however, one or both new countries may legislate small to major changes in its participation in the coalition, as any other member of the coalition may do at any time of their choosing. It is important to examine examples such as Afghanistan because different opinions for military objectives are some of the reasons for the difficulties facing this nation. The adoption of the amendment will allow better military actions in concert with citizens' security, beliefs, needs, and desires.

Keep in mind, the proposed amendment divides the country nearly equally. The bases and facilities for each branch of the armed forces are generally evenly spread across the United States. Therefore, and equitable division of military facilities would be simply to have each facility be part of their new country based on the state in which the facility is currently located.

Earlier in the book I discussed the role of the United States administration after the proposed amendment was ratified. The president, cabinet, and national security personal will be still in office during the transitional period after the ratification of the amendment, but their authority will be greatly changed. They will not be authorized to make new regulations or appointments and there will be no new United States laws would be promulgated. Their only authorization will be to assist in the equitable division of federal assets and liabilities. In this role, they will oversee the realignment of the military so that there will be no lapses in the national defense, and that the assets and liabilities of the military are equally and equitably divided.

All military hardware, weapons, and other real property and resources should be divided by population, as are the states. This should closely resemble forty seven percent going to the new Red Country and fifty three percent to the new Blue Country. For example, if there are 100 nearly equally equipped nuclear submarines, the Blue Country would choose one and then the Red County would choose one until 47 are possessed by the Red Country and 53 are possessed by the Blue Country. The same process could be used until all the implements for war and defense are equally and equitably distributed. It should be noted that military personnel from each new country will be motivated to ensure a fair division because it affects them directly.

The realignment of military personnel should also not be a problem. Each new country needs to appoint a Joint chief of staff quickly after the proposed amendment is ratified. Current upper echelon admirals and generals are rather numerous. After each is reassigned to the country of their residence, there should be nearly sufficient numbers in each country that can reestablish the assignments for a continuing and complete chain of command. This process would proceed throughout the entire personnel of all branches of the armed forces. Promotions would logically be necessary in each country's new military to close potential gaps in leadership.

For example, let's assume that the aircraft carrier *U.S.S. Ronald Reagan* was assumed by the Red Country and the carrier *U.S.S. Harry S. Truman* was assumed by the Blue country. Each sailor on the Reagan that resided in the new Blue Country would be reassigned to the Truman, and vice versa. It would be a very short time before both carriers would have full complements of qualified personnel from sailors up through and including the captain. The realigned ship's compliment will consist of residents from the country that commands it. Therefore, transfers of personnel at all levels could be done rapidly without the loss of continuous military readiness and effectiveness. In fact, with a little extra care and time, even units in combat could be rearranged according to the two new country residences without a loss of combat effectiveness. Ideally, this process should be implemented by the admirals already in command.

The supply chain will actually not be highly affected by the ratification of the proposed amendment. Nearly all suppliers, large and small, will continue to bid on and produce military resources in accordance with open contracts as it is currently done. In fact, there will be a lot of contract work in-process upon ratification, and that work would continue to completion. All new contracts would be under the jurisdiction of the new country requesting the work to be contracted.

Foreign bases would be reallocated based on mutual agreement and a requirement that the total value for the domestic and foreign bases will be distributed fifty three percent to the new Blue Country and forty seven percent to the new Red Country, as stated previously. Some examples might be:

- The New Red Country and the New Country might share the Germany bases equally.

- The Japanese bases might become totally controlled by the new Blue Country.
- Guantanamo Bay might become totally controlled by the new Red Country.
- Both new Countries might agree to close the South Korean bases and bring the troops home.

Nuclear weapons also need to be considered. I do not know, and I do not want to know, the size and location of our nuclear arsenal or its supply lines. These weapons, supply chain, and delivery systems need to be divided equally and equitably between the Red Country and the Blue Country. I have faith that the outgoing president and his staff will work effectively with the two new country's federal administrations to assure that the division is done timely, fairly, and safely. Nuclear missile submarines will be easier to reassign, but the balance will be more difficult. Additionally, the nuclear football, entrusted to the current president, must be transferred to two new footballs, one for each new sovereign country. Secrecy is imperative for the nuclear weapons division effort.

All current military secrets will be shared with the two new countries. After the ratification of the proposed amendment, each new country would be free develop and maintain its own secrets as each sovereign government determines.

A whole book can be written for the future of the CIA., Homeland Security, and FBI. if the amendment is ratified. The basic need is that all secrets, records, and perhaps key personnel and operatives, should be shared for an appropriate time (a five year period would be consistent with the dual citizenship period) after which each new country should proceed as a sovereign country independent from the other new country, each with its own national security agencies.

Chapter 13

Energy

Future energy development faces great challenges due to an increasing world population, demands for higher standards of living, and demands for less pollution and a much discussed end to fossil fuels. Without energy, the world's entire industrialized infrastructure would collapse; agriculture, transportation, waste collection, information technology, communications and much of the prerequisites that a developed nation takes for granted. A shortage of the energy needed to sustain this infrastructure could lead to a Malthusian catastrophe.

Source: Wikipedia

Our entire standard of living is based entirely of two parts, human beings with the relationships among people and things. All "things," that are sometimes called "creature comforts," are produced with the use of energy from many sources. Without the use of energy we would all be back in the Stone Age. Even then, fire energy was used for heat and essentials like clay pottery. America is the largest user of energy per person in the world. Not surprisingly we also have the highest standard of living in the world. Energy is directly proportional to standard of living. Therefore, next to human relationships, energy is the most important component of our standard of living. It is generally acknowledged that we are both dependant on foreign sources of energy and we that America has no workable national energy policy for the future. For at least the past thirty years Americans have demanded a national energy policy and, to date, we have no adopted plan. Since our federal government is both broke and so broken, no one really expects that we will have a comprehensive and complete national energy plan of any kind, much less a plan that would offer an increased standard of living for future generations.

Why do we not have an energy plan? The largest factor, in my opinion, is that our country is so philosophically divided between Red and Blue thinking people that there are only arguments for future energy programs and no agreements of significance. The only major agreement between the two philosophies is that America needs to be less dependent on foreign energy sources in general, and oil in particular. Even with this basic agreement America grows even more dependent on foreign sources every day. So much for bipartisan progress.

The proposed amendment establishes two new sovereign countries each with vastly different social and political philosophies from the other.   This releases each new country to address the energy issue from two different directions. The Blue Country would reduce its total energy requirements by the use and production of smarter and more efficient energy. They would also emphasize and develop renewable fuel sources in preference to fossil, nuclear fission, and other non-renewable energy sources.

Perhaps the best solution to our growing energy challenges comes from The Union of Concerned Scientists:

"No single solution can meet our society's future energy needs. The solution instead will come from a family of diverse energy technologies that share a common thread -- they do not deplete our natural resources or destroy our environment."

-- Eric McLamb

Nuclear energy is a significant energy source for both the new Blue Country and the new Red Country. It is interesting to note that each new country will have slightly over fifty nuclear reactors currently in use producing about eleven percent of the total energy produced. This also equates to the production of about twenty percent of the electricity in both new countries. The Blue Country, based on its expressed concerns, will most likely phase out the nuclear reactors and replace them with other energy sources. This will require massive and extensive development and building replacement energy producing sources. The Red Country, on the other hand, would see nuclear reactors as a clean, non carbon dioxide producing energy source that is safe, controllable, and reliable. Therefore, it is expected that Red Country would extend the use of nuclear power and would build more nuclear plants. It's obvious from the above that without the amendment being ratified, the question of nuclear energy will not be solved by the current non-functioning, broke and broken, federal government. They will just continue to argue a lot and do nothing.

Ethanol is an energy source that has come and gone. It is an example of politics over practicality. To me, the most significant question for ethanol that should be placed to the operator of an ethanol plant is, "If you use the ethanol you produce to run your plant, how much extra ethanol would have to be able to supply the market?" The answer is, "It takes more energy to run the plant than the ethanol could produce. Therefore, it is impossible to run the plant with the energy produced." The only reason ethanol has been so widely developed is because free money was available, only to adequately politically connected investors, for its development and production from the federal government.

Wind power is actually one of the few energy sources that would be expanded in both the new Red Country and the new Blue Country. However, the development of wind power will, for some time, require extensive government subsidies because the electricity produced is much more expensive than from fossil or nuclear sources. The Blue Country, whose emphasis is more on renewable energy, will place a high priority, and will subsidize heavily, wind energy. In comparison, the Red Country would develop wind energy technology, but will restrict implementation until the energy produced is more cost effective. There are several other renewable energy sources such as hydroelectric, tidal, geothermal, biomass, etc., that all will be developed by both the new countries. By circumventing the current broke, broken, and nonfunctioning federal government, all these new energy sources will be expedited by the new countries.

Natural gas will be considered by both new countries as a clean, viable, economical, and major source of energy for the future. Both countries will have significant domestic resources to develop independent energy sources from natural gas.

Oil is a widely used and essential energy source, and will remain so, for both new countries. Currently, our major supplies of oil are foreign. This is not only a drain on national assets, but it is also a market supplied by many countries that have openly stated they are enemies of the United States. Continuing to expand our reliance on these sources is not practical for the long term. The Blue Country can be expected to reduce its oil dependency on the foreign markets by conservation, efficient use of energy, and the development of alternative and renewable energy sources. The Red Country, in contrast, would be expected to develop their own domestic resources quickly and discontinue foreign purchases over time. Both of these approaches are good because they will reduce the drain of assets from both countries, allowing more funds for the services to be provided to the citizens of each country.

Coal is abundant in the United States and, like the population, is split relatively evenly between both new countries. Again, the Blue Country will be expected to reduce their reliance on coal in preference to renewable energy and efficiencies. The Red Country can be expected to develop coal produced energy until the country is totally independent of foreign energy sources.

Global warming is a hotly debated issue in today's political arena; however, there is not even a general consensus as to whether or not global warming actually exists. The contentious argument is just another example of our government having major debate without action. Both the Red-thinking and Blue thinking people have expressed that, in the long run, the development of alternative energies and conservation will be developed and used. The only real argument is in regards to the speed in which renewable energies will replace fossil fuels and nuclear produced energy.

The above discussion, in my opinion, will produce self-sufficient energy for both new countries and permanently remove dependency on foreign energy sources. This is only possible if the proposed amendment is ratified. However, these two new countries are still part of the world. The world has, and will continue, to greatly expand their use of fossil fuels for its energy. The world's resources for fossil fuels are limited. So, the only debate is how limited? When will they expire? Many people believe that the world can raise it standard of living for all its citizens with totally renewable fuels. This is an admirable goal, but what if it is not possible? After all, it would be the largest development known to civilization.

There is another renewable energy source that has the potential to supply considerably more energy than the world would ever need. This is fusion reactor technology. The key to successful commercial fusion reactors is the use of extremely strong magnets to contain the fusion reaction long enough to extract the energy from the reaction. To make these magnets it is necessary to use super conductive materials. Current technology requires these magnets to be cooled to super-low temperatures which are impractical to maintain. In my opinion, the most significant advance humanity will see will be the creation of super conductive material that can be maintained in the range of 100 to 200 degrees Fahrenheit. The two new countries will each already be among the most technologically advanced countries in the world. As discussed above, each new country will have sound energy policies. If these two countries competed technologically to create ambient temperature super conductive material, the winner would have the ability to solve the world's energy crisis. Such development in our current broke and broken country is impossible.

After the proposed amendment is ratified, there should be no disruption in the electrical energy supply to either new country. Electrical energy production and distribution is all controlled by privately owned companies, most of which already operate in an international market. They are totally capable of cross-billing energy across the new boarders between the new Blue Country and the new Red Country that peacefully share a common electrical grid infrastructure. Also, the power plants are privately owned and fully capable of building the needs determined by each of the two new countries. Therefore, the supply and distribution of energy should have no disruption upon ratification of the proposed amendment.

Chapter 14

Currency and Monetary Responsibility

As authorized by the constitutions of both new countries, each country will issue their individually sovereign currency. For five years, the two currencies will be exchangeable at a 1:1 ratio with the current U.S. dollar. The new currency should be issued and exchanged, dollar for dollar, with the old U.S. dollar until there are no more old U.S. dollars. This exchange should be completed within the first five years after the ratification of the amendment. I would discourage both countries from forming a common currency modeled after the Euro used in much of Europe. We are a much divided country and monetary policy for Blue thinking people is vastly different that the monetary policy for Red-thinking people. The Blue progressive idea for monetary issues is that money should be controlled by a strong central government so that all society has equal access to and use of the countries money. The Red philosophy is more conservative in the use of money. They will rely heavily on the free competitive market to equitably distribute money throughout the economy. I contend that the progressive philosophy will best serve the new Blue Country. Additionally, I contend that and that the new Red Country will use the conservative approach as the best system for the Red Country. It should be obvious that the reverse of these policies will not work. In other words, "vice versa" doesn't apply this time.

I also contend that the fight over monetary policy in Washington D.C. between the Red-thinking leaders and the Blue thinking leaders is one of the main causes that has broken Washington D.C. and has left this country broke. It is also logical to assume that the world exchange rates will differ significantly between dollars for a Blue based government when compared to dollars from a

Red based government. Both the new countries will benefit from separate currencies, exchange rates, and monetary policies.

The current national debt must also be addressed. I think that the only equitable action is that each new county assume the debt on a population basis. Specifically, the 15 trillion dollar debt should be divided forty seven percent to be assumed by the new Red Country. Likewise, fifty three percent should be assumed by the new Blue Country. This division is prorated in accordance with the 2010 national census as shown in appendix D. Each country must then develop a strategy to pay down, keep fixed, or expand their debt according to their national objectives. Additionally, each new country will need to develop a Federal Reserve organization soon after the proposed amendment is ratified in order to quickly get stability for the currency and implement a monetary policy consistent with the requirements determined by the two new country's federal governments.

Hard commodities held by the current federal government such as gold, silver, and other strategic reserves should also be divided by the same population of the forty seven percent and the fifty three percent rule. Oops! The silver reserves have already been sold off by the broke and broken current federal government. The oil reserves cannot be easily moved, but the value split for each new Country can be handled with good accounting. What's next if the proposed amendment is not adopted? We don't really need a gold reserve do we? Again the difference of opinions between the Blue philosophy and the Red philosophy are diametrically opposed. Only the proposed amendment will let both the Blue thought and the Red thought be exercised. Who is really right? Actually both Red and Blue philosophies have a basis that would succeed if promoted separately and by leaders with sympathetic views. Again, "live and let live" also applies to financial issues.

Chapter 15

The Future of the Political Parties

"An association of men who will not quarrel with one another is a thing which has never yet existed, from the greatest confederacy of nations down to a town meeting or a vestry"
- Thomas Jefferson

We are a country that considers itself a "two party" country, namely the Democrat Party and the Republican Party. In this book I have stressed "Blue Thinking" and "Red-thinking" people instead of Democrats and Republicans. Each of these political parties is a coalition of people that present candidates for the citizens to vote for to fill elected offices from local, county, and state elections, including the election of the U.S. president, U.S. House of Representatives and the U.S. Senate. Chapter 1 describes "Red" and "Blue" thinking people as two groups of Americans that have very different ideas as to how this country should be run in general, with an emphasis on their opposing demands for the future performance of the federal government.

It is generally considered that only thirty-five percent of the voting public consider themselves members of the Democratic Party, about thirty percent of voters consider themselves Republicans, and about three percent are members of various "third party" political parties that have specific parochial agendas. That leaves a balance of about thirty-two percent of the voting public as "independents" who normally choose to vote for a Republican or Democrat candidate they like best. According to most pundits today, the independents generally vote for the least offensive candidate instead of the best qualified candidate. This fact is why most national office candidates find negative advertising against the opponent as more effective in elections than their positive stands on the issues and their qualifications.

Now consider that less than half of the qualified voters in America actually vote. I call them the "politically apathetic majority." They are either too disgusted with, and or see no hope for, a broke and broken America (chapter 2) so why vote? Or, maybe most of the politically apathetic citizens just do not believe their vote counts so they just ignore politics and hope their daily lives are not affected by the politicians. "Stay below the radar" is a common phrase among the apathetic. Over the years, I have met a lot of people that do not vote, and, from my experience, they all have strong personal opinions and beliefs for not only their own daily lives, but also for the future of themselves, their families and their communities. Nevertheless, even among the politically apathetic, people are not neutral. They are either "Blue" or "Red" in their personal beliefs.

Democrats are mostly "Blue" thinking people and pursue "Blue" ideals. The states where the blue candidates occupy a majority of the elected offices are generally referred to as "Blue States" as discussed in this book. They truly believe, and for good reason, that America would be a better country if "Blue" thought prevailed to a greater extent. "Blue" thinking people elect Democrats with a mandate to expanded the federal government to better provide social justice and equality to all the citizens.

On the other hand, Republicans are mostly just the opposite of the Democrats. They are generally "Red" thinking people who believe, and for good reason, that America would be a better country if the federal government was greatly reduced in size, operated within its income, and that the states and local governments should have the greatest influence on the country.

Keep in mind, this country is divided geographically as well as ideologically along blue and red-thinking people as illustrated in this book as red and blue states. It is interesting to note that all Republicans are not Red-thinking. The New England states are generally recognized as more progressive and Blue thinking than the rest of the country. Similarly, the Republican Congresspersons and Senators from New England, as few as they are, are actually more committed to Blue ideology than to Red ideology. Actually, this is a good thing because these blue thinking Republicans are actually representing the majority of their constituents who think blue. The opposite is true among elected Democrats at the national level. Stay with me on the next sentences as colors get to be confusing. The Democrat leaders in Washington have identified "Blue dog" Democrats that frequently side with "Red" committed Republicans on many social and fiscal national issues. Most of these "Blue dog" Democrats actually are more "Red" in their thinking than "Blue." This is also a good thing. These "Blue dog" Democrats mostly represent districts and states that have more Red-thinking constituents than Blue thinking constituents. Thus, based on the above the division of America into two sovereign countries, as presented in the proposed Constitutional amendment, is geographically well founded.

There are two appendices that are worthy of study. appendix B shows what the new countries' House of Representatives would consist of with current representatives in office. appendix B shows what the new countries' senates would consist of with current senators in office. A study of these appendices will show that a large majority of the new Red Country House and Senate will be Republican with some Red-leaning Democrats. Further, these show that the new Blue Country house and senate will have a large Democrat membership with some Blue-leaning Republicans.

Please consider that the ratification of the proposed amendment will not be simply a division of Democrats and Republicans. The amendment, and its ratification, is much more profound as it allows like-minded citizens to participate in, and live with, a government that is agreeable to the beliefs and expectations of a vast majority of its citizens. There will still be two dominate political parties in both new countries. The two new parties will most likely not be named as Democrat and Republican parties. The priorities of the new parties will change a lot. In the new Blue Country, both the new parties will both move more to a blue thinking social justice emphasis (commonly referred to as a move to the political left). The new Red Country political parties will "move more to the right." Today, such realignment of the government and political parties is impossible. The process demands political warfare between red and blue ideals with one side victorious and wielding the power to force the other side to accept laws and regulations repugnant to the losing side as discussed in detail in chapter 2.

The amendment and its ratification will peacefully address the political problems of the day and circumvent the broke and broken condition in Washington D.C. It will not be, nor should it be expected to be, a panacea of politically peaceful discourse. It does, however, promote heated discussion of like-minded people with common goals in government. "Live and let live" is, in my opinion, the best solution to today's problems with Washington D.C. and a divided Blue versus Red country. Thomas Jefferson summed up perfectly what the two new countries will see politically:

Chapter 16

Other Issues

"An association of men who will not quarrel with one another is a thing which has never yet existed, from the greatest confederacy of nations down to a town meeting or a vestry."

- Thomas Jefferson

There are twelve issues that are highly sensitive today that would be much easier to address after the proposed amendment is ratified. There are major differences of opinions on these issues between those with Red thought and those with Blue thought. However, in the Red community there is broad consensus as to what should be done with each of the following issues. This is likewise true among people with Blue thoughts and principles. The bottom line is that there will be more freedom of actions for all concerned.

Balanced Budget

A balanced budget is a very important issue. This issue can only be settled with a constitutional amendment. The reason this issue is so important is because Red-thinking people and Blue thinking people are fundamentally different and this issue is equally important to both. Blue thinking people truly believe that the federal government should be expanded in order to create a better society. This will require the federal government to gain a larger portion of the national economy. Therefore, a balanced budget that limits government growth is totally unacceptable. Red-thinking people truly believe that the federal government must be reduced and governance responsibility placed closer to the states and the people. Therefore, only a balanced budget that will reduce, or limit, the size of the federal government will be acceptable. It is clear that our broke and broken Washington D.C. will not solve the balanced budget issue. With a grid locked congress there will be insufficient support to propose an amendment for the states to ratify. If the elite Fifteen in Washington D.C. (chapter 2) become all Red-thinking leaders, a balanced budget amendment will most likely be a high priority, and when ratified, would further divide this country because half of America is comprised of Blue thinking people that will not like that amendment. My proposed amendment, initiated by the states themselves, would allow Red-thinking people and Blue thinking people to both have what they desire without forcing their beliefs on each other.

Term Limits

Term Limits is also a very important issue. This issue can only be settled with a constitutional amendment. The reason this issue is so important is because Red thinking people and Blue thinking people are fundamentally different and this issue is equally important to both. Red-thinking people believe in a smaller federal government and expect their elected officials to be directly associated with state and local issues. They feel that government would be better served if the elected officials knew that they would return to the society and live under the laws that they helped pass. Blue thinking people, on the other hand, expect the federal government to be much more in control of society and would depend on career proven leaders as their elected officials. Many states, mostly of Red thinking people, have enacted term limits for their state governments. These term limits have, in the opinions of those states, greatly enhanced the quality of their elected state officials. Prior amendments to the constitution have been initiated in congress. It is clear to see that since the country is evenly divided, congress cannot and will not institute a term limits amendment to the constitution. However, when the proposed amendment is ratified it will be expected that the new Red Country would impose term limits on its federally elected officials. Conversely, the Blue Country will not consider such an amendment to be necessary. Therefore, the proposed amendment would solve the term limits issue as no other process can do.

Abortion

It is very easy to conclude that the new Red Country, with a majority of Red thinking people, will promote pro-life laws and restrict the use of abortions. It is equally easy to conclude that the new Blue Country, with a large majority of Blue thinking citizens, would expand abortion rights making abortion easily available to all those who make this choice. The major current political war of conscience would be greatly diffused with the ratification of the proposed amendment, and the vast majority of citizens in both countries would be satisfied with the results.

Taxes

Remember that all current tax laws will apply to both new countries immediately after the proposed amendment is ratified. The new Blue Country would adopt new tax laws that would equalize the ability to pay taxes consistent with the needs of the general population. They would use tax law to address the excessive profits from corporations and from the very wealthy. The collected taxes would be used to better prioritize use of national funds for national purposes. One expected action of the new Red Country is to reduce the size of their federal government and place more of society's responsibilities onto individual state governments. Therefore, the Red Country will, most likely, reduce the taxes for federal use in line with the reduction of services provided. Obviously these are two major differences in tax philosophy. Only a ratification of the proposed amendment would allow both of these philosophies to be enacted, and this would be respected by the vast majority of all Americans.

States Rights

The Red thinking people truly believe that the best government is the government closest to the people. They also believe the constitution restricts the federal government from activities reserved for the states. Therefore, the new Red Country would restrain its federal government and let the individual states have more jurisdiction over daily life. On the other hand, the new Blue Country would continue to expand federal government control over the country in order to guarantee equal rights, benefits, and obligations among all residents in all states. Only the ratification of the proposed amendment would permit these two divergent philosophies to flourish to the satisfaction of Red and Blue thinking people. The "politically apathetic majority" in both countries will be able to continue their daily life without concern as to the details of the federal and state governments, just they are currently doing now; however, the politically apathetic majority will be happier with federal governments that work and that are not broke and broken.

Education

In the 1950s, the United States was acknowledged as having the best educational system in the world. Now, it has deteriorated to a level that is below the average for developed nations. Blue thinking people endorse expanded central government control to advance education. It would be successful in increasing responsiveness to student concerns, a broader emphasis on social concerns, and guarantees that every student would get the best education that the student can obtain. Blue thinking people feel thwarted by Red thinking resistance that prevents the development of their educational plans. Red thinking people, on the other hand, feel that education would be greatly enhanced if more control was delegated to the local school districts and the parents of the students. Red-thinking people also believe that competitive ideas among private and public schools would enhance the overall educational system. I truly believe that both of these systems could elevate the educational achievement of American students if they could be implemented. This can be done if the proposed amendment was ratified. Then the Blue thinking people can institute their educational policy without restraints from Red thinking people, and vice versa. If the status quo continues, the educational system will continue to deteriorate and will be detrimental to all of us, especially our children. I firmly believe that ratification of the proposed amendment is the best way to get desperately needed reform that will again have Americans as the best educated people in the world.

Public Unions

Public unions are currently contentious and becoming more demanding as the country continues to be more polarized and divided. It is evident that Blue thinking people prefer to have group representation in the form of unions to better protect and preserve their ability to earn a living. The new Blue Country will most likely embrace the public unions as the necessary organization to assure that all public employees are treated fairly and in harmony with their private employee counterparts. Much of the current public union dissatisfaction is associated with inequities between states. This will be solved with the expanded federal government of the new Blue Country. The new Red Country will most likely endorse the majority of Red thinking people who would prefer the freedom of individuals to negotiate their own working conditions, wages, and benefits with their employers. This thought would follow though for both private and public employees in the new Red Country.

The above would address most of the current discord of public employees at the state level. The proposed amendment facilitates the "live and let live" principle and enables both sides to win.

Religion

Religion is a highly debated national issue. The main conflict centers over the interpretation of the constitution concerning the separation of church and state. Rather than discuss the pros and cons, I would prefer to simply give some examples of what I would expect to occur in the new Red Country and the new Blue Country after the ratification of the proposed amendment.

Expected Blue Country Actions:

- All historical references to, and preferences for, Judeo-Christian philosophy would be removed from all government activity so that no person will be offended by government action.
- All religions would be protected under the law even if they oppose the actions of the federal government.
- The quotation "...Under God" will be removed from the Pledge of Allegiance, as well as "In God We Trust" from all currency and public buildings.

Expected Red Country Actions:

- The nation would be proclaimed as a "Christian" nation, because that is representative of its heritage and the vast majority of its people.

- All religious and non-religious beliefs will be protected as long as inter-religious relations are peaceful and abide by the laws of the country.
- Public schools would be allowed to institute school prayer and tolerate religious discussion.

After reading the above points, anyone can understand why this is one more example of a country that is permanently polarized and in need of the ratification of the proposed amendment.

Morality

Individual morality is actually one of the strongest differences between Blue thinking and Red thinking people. Just consider the mutual contempt between the "Bible Belt," which is mostly Red thinking people, and the "Progressive," which are mostly Blue thinking people. The Bible Belt will be almost totally in the new Red Country. Their thinking is fundamentally different than the Progressive expressions associated with California and Northern cities like New York, Chicago, and Detroit. A significant amount of activity in Washington D.C. is to create new legislation to permit freedoms for Blue thinking people which are considered immoral by Red thinking people. Consider this: Blue thinking people would typically be just as irritated with the federal government if they suddenly passed a law mandating prayer in public schools, right? Red thinking people typically would support such legislation. Once again, the ratification of the proposed amendment would permit Blue thinking people, who would be the vast majority in the new Blue Country, to obtain legislation compatible with their lifestyles. Similarly, the Red Country would pass laws that would be compatible with Red thinking people's morality. Another example would be that the Red Country would adopt a law that marriage can only be between one man and one woman, whereas the Blue

Country would allow any consenting adults the right to marry regardless of religion, race, creed, or sexual orientation.

Media

Both the current and the two new proposed constitutions will equally guarantee freedom of the press and media. The ratification of the proposed amendment makes no demands or requires any changes concerning free press. After the ratification of the amendment the free press is actually more "free" to report news and comment on issues as they would no longer have responsibility to take sides between Red thinking and Blue thinking people.

Political Apathy

There is a large portion of Americans that are considered "politically apathetic." These people are convinced they can do nothing to change current events, so they just live with it and do the best they can under their given circumstances. Apathy, in many cases, is simply an acknowledgement that they are satisfied with the political status quo. Many of these politically apathetic Americans could care less about their government as long as they are "just left alone." The ratification of the proposed amendment will not create any additional discomfort to politically apathetic people. In fact, they may be more satisfied when the broke and broken current government is replaced by two viable, active, and mutually respected governments. This might actually motivate the otherwise politically apathetic person be more responsive to news about their government and issues that may directly affect them personally.

Declaration of War

This is a huge concern for nearly all citizens. Both Red and Blue thinking people agree on a strong defense and the protection of all our people. If the proposed amendment is ratified, both countries will have very strong defensive militaries with common goals. It is obvious that both new Countries will agree that an attack on one would be interpreted as an attack on the other. This is one of the few areas where I believe "common sense" will protect us all.

If the current United States continues to become more divided and encounters a major economic collapse, as predicted by many, there will be an enormous increase of hostilities among individuals. This would extend all the way to the top of government. If this occurs, the only recourse between Blue thinking and Red thinking people would be open civil war, which is unacceptable for both sides. Civil war, as we have seen in many countries, results in untold destruction and misery. Even today secession is an ever-increasing subject in political discourse. This is because nothing else appears to be able to correct our broke and broken federal government. The ratification of this amendment before and economic collapse would ensure a peaceful transition, prevent open civil war, and provide a means for both Red and Blue philosophies to develop viable federal governments in conformance with their beliefs.

Chapter 17

Summary and Call For Action

The United States is at a critical crossroads today. The people and our American society are the most advanced, prosperous, and powerful nation in the world today; however, our federal government is both broke financially and broken as a functioning national government. The current federal spending is the highest level ever and is being propped up with about forty percent of borrowed money. Even so, federal spending is forecasted to significantly increase every year for years to come. The approval rating of the Congress and Senate is below twenty percent and dropping. The approval of the administration's performance is not much better. Washington D.C. is amuck with contentious rhetoric, overwhelming special interest groups demanding (and getting) more from the government, a gridlocked legislature and an administration that cannot even present a budget for the current year, much less for the future. Washington D.C.'s dysfunction and a debt in excess of $14,000,000,000,000.00 cast an ever darkening cloud over the future of the United States. The last ten years in particular show that Washington D.C. cannot and will not restructure itself to repair the broke and broken government it created. The time is now for the people to take action.

The real reason for our failing federal government is, in my opinion, that the people of this great nation are so evenly and strongly divided between two completely different philosophies that the present federal government system cannot do anything that will not reward one philosophy while angering the other half, and the division widens. One philosophy, referred to as "Blue" in his book, demands that the federal government take a larger role in the control and government over all states. This way all the people will have equal protection under the law, equal social justice, and equal access to the goods produced by the country. The other philosophy, referred to as "Red" in this book, demands that a smaller and less intrusive federal government. This way an open, free, and competitive market will produce the greatest growth in the economy of a country which will raise the standard of living for all of its people. It is unreasonable to expect the country's division to repair itself. Left to the current course of events, the division will only widen with time. It is commonly agreed that this continuing division among the American people will be detrimental to all, and the government cannot stop a continual decline in the American dream.

The idea of dividing the country along philosophical lines is a path that would simply acknowledge the differences we have in America and would allow each separate philosophy to follow their dreams and aspirations without the constraints and objections of the opposite philosophy. This would transform our current ever-increasing political fighting for power into two separate countries. Each country would pursue their individual plans for the future. People with common goals and purposes can accomplish amazing things. Remember, it is not that either the Red or Blue philosophy is right or wrong, it is that the fight between them is wrong. The ratification of the proposed amendment would allow peace and harmony within the two new countries. "Live and let live" is a good policy.

Among the many issues discussed in this book, please take particular note of two particularly divisive and important issues for all Americans. First, for Blue leaning Obama Care, there are twenty-seven Red-leaning states suing the federal government to repeal this legislation. Secondly, all the Red-leaning states that pass immigration reform are being sued by the Blue leaning federal administration. There are at least twenty-seven states that have passed, or are in the process of passing, Red leaning immigration legislation. The fact that there are so many states suing the federal government, and the federal government suing the states on the two largest issues of the day, speaks volumes. When two entities that are supposed to be "married" in governance are suing each other, it's time for a divorce decree, don't you think?

Please consider this book carefully. If you believe that the proposed amendment should be developed by a constitutional convention called by the states, please contact your local, state, and federal representatives and encourage them to read this book. After all, this country is a country by and for the people, and the proposed amendment and its process for ratification is constitutional. It is your duty and right as an American to insist on the government you want

Part IV:
Appendices

Appendix A
New Red Country and New Blue Country Map

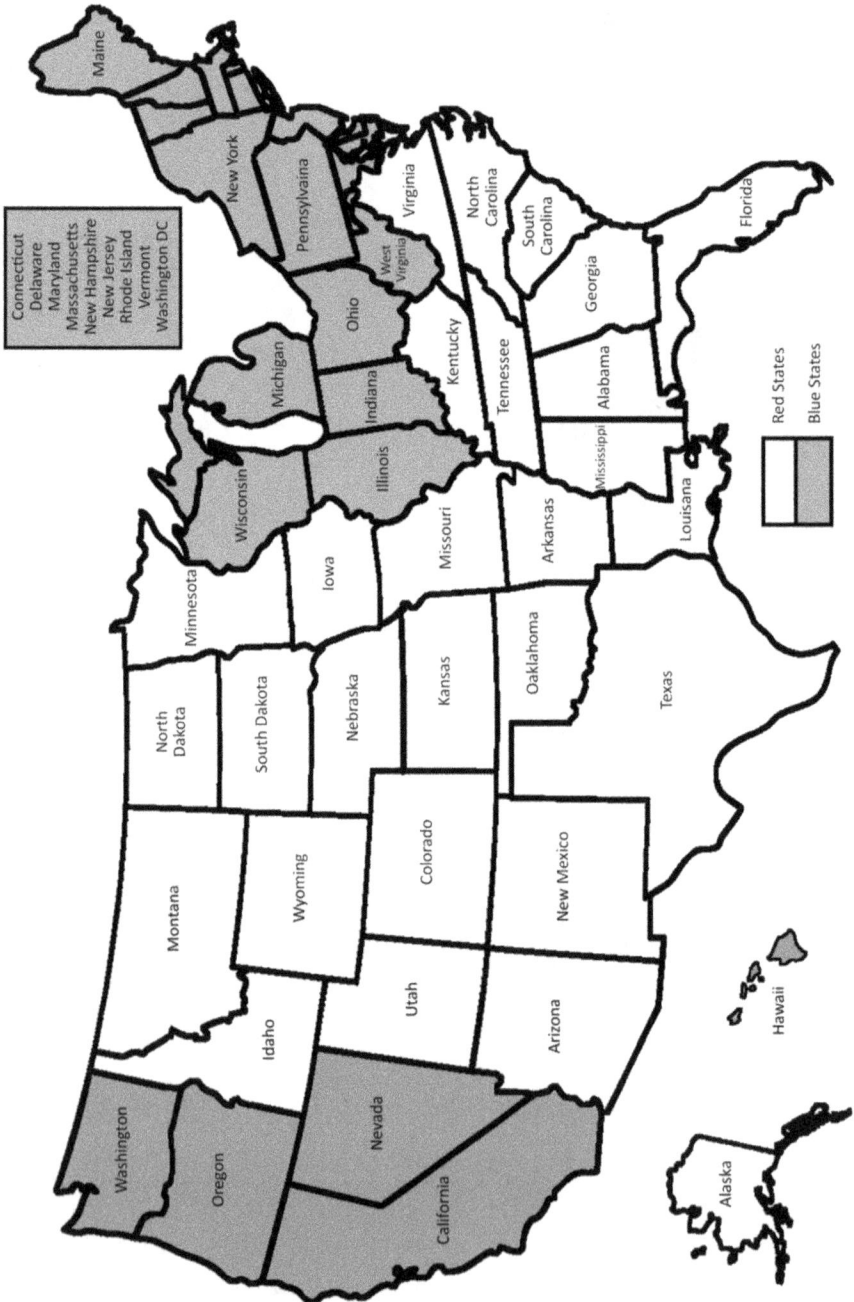

Appendix B
New Country House of Representatives

Blue Country House of Representatives		Red Country House of Representatives	
Congressperson	Party	Congressperson	Party
California		*Alabama*	
Thompson, Mike	D	Bonner, Jo	R
Herger, Wally	R	Roby, Martha	R
Lungren, Daniel E.	R	Rogers (AL), Mike	R
McClintock, Tom	R	Aderholt, Robert	R
Matsui, Doris O.	D	Brooks, Mo	R
Woolsey, Lynn	D	Bachus, Spencer	R
Miller, George	D	Sewell, Terri A.	D
Pelosi, Nancy	D		
Lee, Barbara	D	*Alaska*	
Garamendi, John	D	Young, Don	R
McNerney, Jerry	D		
Speier, Jackie	D	**Arizona * Plus 1**	
Stark, Fortney Pete	D	Gosar, Paul R.	R
Eshoo, Anna G.	D	Flake, Jeff	R
Honda, Mike	D	Quayle, Ben	R
Lofgren, Zoe	D	Pastor, Ed	D
Farr, Sam	D	Schweikert, David	R
Cardoza, Dennis	D	Flake, Jeff	R
Denham, Jeff	R	Grijalva, Raul	D
Costa, Jim	D	Giffords, Gabrielle	D
Nunes, Devin	R		
McCarthy, Kevin	R	*Arkansas*	
Capps, Lois	D	Crawford, Rick	R
Gallegly, Elton	R	Griffin, Tim	R
McKeon, Buck	R	Womack, Steve	R
Dreier, David	R	Ross, Mike	D
Sherman, Brad	D		
Berman, Howard	D	*Colorado*	
Schiff, Adam	D	DeGette, Diana	D
Waxman, Henry	D	Polis, Jared	D
Becerra, Xavier	D	Tipton, Scott	R
Chu, Judy	D	Gardner, Cory	R
Bass, Karen	D	Lamborn, Doug	R
Roybal-Allard, Lucille	D	Coffman, Mike	R
Waters, Maxine	D	Perlmutter, Ed	D
Harman, Jane -- Vacancy	D		

Richardson, Laura	D	**Florida* Plus 2**		
Napolitano, Grace	D	Miller, Jeff	R	
Sanchez, Linda	D	Southerland, Steve	R	
Royce, Ed	R	Brown, Corrine	D	
Lewis, Jerry	R	Crenshaw, Ander	R	
Miller, Gary	R	Nugent, Richard	R	
Baca, Joe	D	Stearns, Cliff	R	
Calvert, Ken	R	Mica, John	R	
Bono, Mary	R	Webster, Daniel	R	
Rohrabacher, Dana	R	Bilirakis, Gus M.	R	
Sanchez, Loretta	D	Young, C.W. Bill	R	
Campbell, John	R	Castor, Kathy	D	
Issa, Darrell	R	Ross, Dennis	R	
Bilbray, Brian P.	R	Buchanan, Vern	R	
Filner, Bob	D	Mack, Connie	R	
Hunter, Duncan D.	R	Posey, Bill	R	
Davis, Susan	D	Rooney, Tom	R	
		Wilson, Frederica	D	
Connecticut		Ros-Lehtinen, Ileana	R	
Larson, John B.	D	Deutch, Ted	D	
Courtney, Joe	D	Wasserman Schultz, Debbie	D	
DeLauro, Rosa L.	D	Diaz-Balart, Mario	R	
Himes, Jim	D	West, Allen	R	
Murphy, Christopher S.	D	Hastings, Alcee L.	D	
		Adams, Sandy	R	
Delaware		Rivera, David	R	
Carney, John	D			
		Georgia * Plus 1		
District of Columbia		Kingston, Jack	R	
Norton, Eleanor Holmes	D	Bishop Jr., Sanford D.	D	
		Westmoreland, Lynn A.	R	
Hawaii		Johnson, Henry C. Jr.	D	
Hanabusa, Colleen	D	Lewis, John	D	
Hirono, Mazie K.	D	Price, Tom	R	
		Woodall, Robert	R	
Illinois * Minus 1		Scott, Austin	R	
Rush, Bobby L.	D	Graves, Tom	R	
Jackson Jr., Jesse L.	D	Broun, Paul C.	R	
Lipinski, Daniel	D	Gingrey, Phil	R	
Gutierrez, Luis	D	Barrow, John	D	
Quigley, Mike	D	Scott, David	D	
Roskam, Peter J.	R			
Davis, Danny K.	D	**Idaho**		
Walsh, Joe	R	Labrador, Raul R.	R	
Schakowsky, Jan	D	Simpson, Mike	R	

Dold, Robert	R
Kinzinger, Adam	R
Costello, Jerry	D
Biggert, Judy	R
Hultgren, Randy	R
Johnson, Timothy V.	R
Manzullo, Donald	R
Schilling, Bobby	R
Schock, Aaron	R
Shimkus, John	R

Indiana

Visclosky, Peter	D
Donnelly, Joe	D
Stutzman, Marlin	R
Rokita, Todd	R
Burton, Dan	R
Pence, Mike	R
Carson, André	D
Bucshon, Larry	R
Young, Todd	R

Maine

Pingree, Chellie	D
Michaud, Michael	D

Maryland

Harris, Andy	R
Ruppersberger, Dutch	D
Sarbanes, John P.	D
Edwards, Donna F.	D
Hoyer, Steny H.	D
Bartlett, Roscoe	R
Cummings, Elijah	D
Van Hollen, Chris	D

Massachusetts * Minus 1

Olver, John	D
Neal, Richard E.	D
McGovern, James	D
Frank, Barney	D
Tsongas, Niki	D
Tierney, John	D
Markey, Ed	D
Capuano, Michael E.	D

Iowa * Minus 1

Braley, Bruce L.	D
Loebsack, David	D
Boswell, Leonard	D
Latham, Tom	R
King, Steve	R

Kansas

Huelskamp, Tim	R
Jenkins, Lynn	R
Yoder, Kevin	R
Pompeo, Mike	R

Kentucky

Whitfield, Ed	R
Guthrie, S. Brett	R
Yarmuth, John A.	D
Davis, Geoff	R
Rogers, Harold	R
Chandler, Ben	D

Louisiana * Minus 1

Scalise, Steve	R
Richmond, Cedric	D
Landry, Jeffrey	R
Fleming, John	R
Alexander, Rodney	R
Cassidy, William	R
Boustany Jr., Charles W.	R

Minnesota

Walz, Timothy J.	D
Kline, John	R
Paulsen, Erik	R
McCollum, Betty	D
Ellison, Keith	D
Bachmann, Michele	R
Peterson, Collin C.	D
Cravaack, Chip	R

Mississippi

Nunnelee, Alan	R
Thompson, Bennie G.	D
Harper, Gregg	R
Palazzo, Steven	R

Lynch, Stephen F.	D
Keating, William	D

Michigan * Minus 1

Benishek, Dan	R
Huizenga, Bill	R
Amash, Justin	R
Camp, Dave	R
Kildee, Dale	D
Upton, Fred	R
Walberg, Tim	R
Rogers (MI), Mike	R
Peters, Gary	D
Miller, Candice	R
McCotter, Thaddeus	R
Levin, Sander	D
Clarke, Hansen	D
Conyers Jr., John	D
Dingell, John	D

Nevada * Plus 1

Berkley, Shelley	D
Heller, Dean -- Vacancy	R
Heck, Joe	R

New Hampshire

Guinta, Frank	R
Bass, Charles	R

New Jersey * Minus 1 D

Andrews, Robert E.	R
LoBiondo, Frank	R
Runyan, Jon	R
Smith, Chris	R
Garrett, Scott	D
Pallone Jr., Frank	R
Lance, Leonard	D
Pascrell Jr., Bill	D
Rothman, Steven	D
Payne, Donald M.	R
Frelinghuysen, Rodney	D
Holt, Rush	D
Sires, Albio	

New York * Minus 2

Missouri * Minus 1

Clay Jr., William	D
Akin, Todd	R
Carnahan, Russ	D
Hartzler, Vicky	R
Cleaver, Emanuel	D
Graves, Sam	R
Long, Billy	R
Emerson, Jo Ann	R
Luetkemeyer, Blaine	R

Montana

Rehberg, Dennis	R

Nebraska

Fortenberry, Jeff	R
Terry, Lee	R
Smith, Adrian	R

New Mexico

Heinrich, Martin T.	D
Pearce, Steve	R
Lujan, Ben R.	D

North Carolina

Butterfield, G.K.	D
Ellmers, Renee	R
Jones, Walter B.	R
Price, David	D
Foxx, Virginia	R
Coble, Howard	R
McIntyre, Mike	D
Kissell, Larry	D
Myrick, Sue	R
McHenry, Patrick T.	R
Shuler, Heath	D
Watt, Mel	D
Miller, Brad	D

North Dakota

Berg, Rick	R

Oklahoma

Sullivan, John	R

Bishop, Timothy	D
Israel, Steve	D
King, Pete	R
McCarthy, Carolyn	D
Ackerman, Gary	D
Meeks, Gregory W.	D
Crowley, Joseph	D
Nadler, Jerrold	D
Weiner, Anthony D.	D
Towns, Edolphus	D
Clarke, Yvette D.	D
Velázquez, Nydia M.	D
Grimm, Michael	R
Maloney, Carolyn	D
Rangel, Charles B.	D
Serrano, José E.	D
Engel, Eliot	D
Lowey, Nita	D
Hayworth, Nan	R
Gibson, Chris	R
Tonko, Paul D.	D
Hinchey, Maurice	D
Owens, Bill	D
Hanna, Richard	R
Buerkle, Ann Marie	R
Lee, Christopher-Vacancy	R
Higgins, Brian	D
Slaughter, Louise	D
Reed, Tom	R

Ohio * Minus 2

Chabot, Steve	R
Schmidt, Jean	R
Turner, Michael	R
Jordan, Jim	R
Latta, Robert E.	R
Johnson, Bill	R
Austria, Steve	R
Boehner, John A.	R
Kaptur, Marcy	D
Kucinich, Dennis J.	D
Fudge, Marcia L.	D
Tiberi, Pat	R
Sutton, Betty	D
LaTourette, Steven C.	R

Boren, Dan	D
Lucas, Frank	R
Cole, Tom	R
Lankford, James	R

South Carolina *Plus 1

Scott, Tim	R
Wilson, Joe	R
Duncan, Jeff	R
Gowdy, Trey	R
Mulvaney, Mick	R
Clyburn, James E.	D

South Dakota

Noem, Kristi	R

Tennessee

Roe, Phil	R
Duncan Jr., John J.	R
Fleischmann, Chuck	R
DesJarlais, Scott	R
Cooper, Jim	D
Black, Diane	R
Blackburn, Marsha	R
Fincher, Stephen	R
Cohen, Steve	D

Texas * Plus 4

Gohmert, Louie	R
Poe, Ted	R
Johnson, Sam	R
Hall, Ralph M.	R
Hensarling, Jeb	R
Barton, Joe	R
Culberson, John	R
Brady, Kevin	R
Green, Al	D
McCaul, Michael T.	R
Conaway, K. Michael	R
Granger, Kay	R
Thornberry, Mac	R
Paul, Ron	R
Hinojosa, Rubén	D
Reyes, Silvestre	D
Flores, Bill	R

Stivers, Steve	R		Jackson Lee, Sheila	D
Renacci, Jim	R		Neugebauer, Randy	R
Ryan, Tim	D		Gonzalez, Charlie A.	D
Gibbs, Bob	R		Smith, Lamar	R
			Olson, Pete	R
Oregon	D		Canseco, Francisco	R
Wu, David	R		Marchant, Kenny	R
Walden, Greg	D		Doggett, Lloyd	D
Blumenauer, Earl	D		Burgess, Michael	R
DeFazio, Peter	D		Farenthold, Blake	R
Schrader, Kurt			Cuellar, Henry	D
			Green, Gene	D
Pennsylvania * Minus 1			Johnson, Eddie Bernice	D
Brady, Robert	D		Carter, John	R
Fattah, Chaka	D		Sessions, Pete	R
Kelly, Mike	R			
Altmire, Jason	D		**Utah * Plus 1**	
Thompson, Glenn W.	R		Bishop, Rob	R
Gerlach, Jim	R		Matheson, Jim	D
Meehan, Pat	R		Chaffetz, Jason	R
Fitzpatrick, Michael G.	R			
Shuster, Bill	R		**Virginia**	
Marino, Tom	R		Wittman, Robert J.	R
Barletta, Lou	R		Rigell, E.	R
Critz, Mark	D		Scott, Robert C.	D
Schwartz, Allyson Y.	D		Forbes, J. Randy	R
Doyle, Mike	D		Hurt, Robert	R
Dent, Charles W.	R		Goodlatte, Bob	R
Pitts, Joseph R.	R		Cantor, Eric	R
Holden, Tim	D		Moran, James	D
Murphy, Tim	R		Griffith, Morgan	R
Platts, Todd	R		Wolf, Frank	R
			Connolly, Gerald E.	D
Rhode Island				
Cicilline, David	D		**Wyoming**	
Langevin, Jim	D		Lummis, Cynthia M.	R
Vermont			*See bottom of table for summary*	
Welch, Peter	D			
Washington * Plus 1				
Inslee, Jay	D			
Larsen, Rick	D			
Herrera Beutler, Jaime	R			
Hastings, Doc	R			

McMorris Rodgers, Cathy	R
Dicks, Norman D.	D
McDermott, Jim	D
Reichert, David G.	R
Smith, Adam	D

West Virginia

McKinley, David	R
Capito, Shelley Moore	R
Rahall, Nick	D

Wisconsin

Ryan, Paul	R
Baldwin, Tammy	D
Kind, Ron	D
Moore, Gwen	D
Sensenbrenner, F. James	R
Petri, Thomas	R
Duffy, Sean P.	R
Ribble, Reid	R

Blue Country Summary:

"R" = Republican Party - "D" = Democrat Party

Total Democrats Elected In 2010 = 134 (57%)

Total Republicans Elected In 2010 = 102 (43%)

Total Congresspersons elected in 2010 = 236

Total for Congress to be elected in 2012 = 229

Note * in 2012 the Blue Country will lose a net of Seven (7) of the current Congresspersons due to the 2010 census reapportionment

Red Country Summary:

"R" = Republican Party - "D" = Democrat Party

Total Democrats Elected In 2010 = 59 (30%)

Total Republicans Elected In 2010 = 139 (70%)

Total Congresspersons elected in 2010 = 198

Total for Congress to be elected in 2012 = 205

Note * in 2012 the Red Country will Gain a net of Seven (7) of the current Congresspersons due to the 2010 census reapportionment

Appendix C
Senators for New Countries

Red Country Senators:

Begich, Mark	(D - AK)
Murkowski, Lisa	(R - AK)
Sessions, Jeff	(R - AL)
Shelby, Richard C.	(R - AL)
Boozman, John	(R - AR)
Pryor, Mark.	(D-AR)
McCain, John	(R - AZ)
Kyl, Jon	(R-AZ)
Bennet, Michael F.	(D - CO)
Udall, Mark	(D - CO)
Nelson, Bill	(D - FL)
Rubio, Marco	(R - FL)
Chambliss, Saxby	(R - GA)
Isakson, Johnny	(R - GA)
Grassley, Chuck	(R - IA)
Harkin, Tom	(D - IA)
Crapo, Mike	(R - ID)
Risch, James E.	(R - ID)
Moran, Jerry	(R - KS)
Roberts, Pat	(R - KS)
McConnell, Mitch	(R - KY)
Paul, Rand	(R - KY)
Landrieu, Mary L.	(D - LA)
Vitter, David	(R - LA)
Franken, Al	(D - MN)
Klobuchar, Amy	(D - MN)
Blunt, Roy	(R - MO)
McCaskill, Claire	(D - MO)
Cochran, Thad	(R - MS)
Wicker, Roger F.	(R - MS)
Baucus, Max	(D - MT)
Tester, Jon	(D - MT)

Blue Country Senators:

Boxer, Barbara	(D - CA)
Feinstein, Dianne	(D - CA)
Blumenthal, Richard	(D - CT)
Lieberman, Joseph I.	(I - CT)
Carper, Thomas R.	(D - DE)
Coons, Christopher A.	(D - DE)
Akaka, Daniel K.	(D - HI)
Inouye, Daniel K.	(D - HI)
Durbin, Richard J.	(D - IL)
Kirk, Mark	(R - IL)
Coats, Daniel	(R - IN)
Lugar, Richard G.	(R - IN)
Brown, Scott P.	(R - MA)
Kerry, John F.	(D - MA)
Cardin, Benjamin L.	(D - MD)
Mikulski, Barbara A.	(D - MD)
Collins, Susan M.	(R - ME)
Snowe, Olympia J.	(R - ME)
Levin, Carl	(D - MI)
Stabenow, Debbie	(D - MI)
Ayotte, Kelly	(R - NH)
Shaheen, Jeanne	(D - NH)
Lautenberg, Frank R.	(D - NJ)
Menendez, Robert	(D - NJ)
Heller, Dean	(R - NV)
Reid, Harry	(D - NV)
Gillibrand, Kirsten E.	(D - NY)
Schumer, Charles E.	(D - NY)
Brown, Sherrod	(D - OH)
Portman, Rob	(R - OH)
Merkley, Jeff	(D - OR)
Wyden, Ron	(D - OR)

Burr, Richard	(R - NC)	Casey, Robert P., Jr.	(D - PA)
Hagan, Kay R.	(D - NC)	Toomey, Patrick J.	(R - PA)
Conrad, Kent	(D - ND)	Reed, Jack	(D - RI)
Hoeven, John	(R - ND)	Whitehouse, Sheldon	(D - RI)
Johanns, Mike	(R - NE)	Leahy, Patrick J.	(D - VT)
Nelson, Ben	(D - NE)	Sanders, Bernard	(I - VT)
Bingaman, Jeff	(D - NM)	Cantwell, Maria	(D - WA)
Udall, Tom	(D - NM)	Murray, Patty	(D - WA)
Coburn, Tom	(R - OK)	Johnson, Ron	(R - WI)
Inhofe, James M.	(R - OK)	Kohl, Herb	(D - WI)
DeMint, Jim	(R - SC)	Manchin, Joe, III	(D - WV)
Graham, Lindsey	(R - SC)	Rockefeller, John D., IV	(D - WV)
Johnson, Tim	(D - SD)		
Thune, John	(R - SD)		
Alexander, Lamar	(R - TN)		
Corker, Bob	(R - TN)		
Cornyn, John	(R - TX)		
Hutchison, Kay Bailey	(R - TX)		
Hatch, Orrin G.	(R - UT)		
Lee, Mike	(R - UT)		
Warner, Mark R.	(D - VA)		
Webb, Jim	(D - VA)		
Barrasso, John	(R - WY)		
Enzi, Michael B.	(R - WY)		

Republicans 11 (25.6%)
Democrats   33 (74.4%)

Republicans 36 (64.3%)
Democrats   20 (35.7%)

Appendix D
State Populations

State	Red Country	Blue Country
Alabama	4,802,982	
Alaska	721,523	
Arizona	6,412,700	
Arkansas	2,926,229	
California		37,341,989
Colorado	5,044,930	
Connecticut		3,581,628
Delaware		900,877
District of Columbia		601723
Florida	18,900,773	
Georgia	9,727,566	
Hawaii		1,366,862
Idaho	1,573,499	
Illinois		12,864,380
Indiana		6,501,582
Iowa	3,053,787	
Kansas	2,863,813	
Kentucky	4,350,606	
Louisiana	4,553,962	
Maine		1,333,074
Maryland		5,789,929
Massachusetts		6,559,644
Michigan		9,911,626
Minnesota	5,314,879	
Mississippi	2,978,240	
Missouri	6,011,478	
Montana	994,416	
Nebraska	1,831,825	
Nevada		2,709,432
New Hampshire		1,321,445

New Jersey		8,807,501
New Mexico	2,067,273	
New York		19,421,055
North Carolina	9,565,781	
North Dakota	675,905	
Ohio		11,568,495
Oklahoma	3,764,882	
Oregon		3,848,606
Pennsylvania		12,734,905
Rhode Island		1,055,247
South Carolina	4,645,975	
South Dakota	819,761	
Tennessee	6,375,431	
Texas	25,268,418	
Utah	2,770,765	
Vermont		630,337
Virginia	8,037,736	
Washington		6,753,369
west Virginia		1,859,815
Wisconsin		5,698,230
Wyoming	568,300	
Totals	**146,623,435**	**163,161,751**
	28 States	22 States
% of national	47.3%	52.7%

Note: District of Columbia was added to Blue Country
Data taken from US 2010 Census Report

Appendix E
World Population Rankings

Country	Population	Date of estimate	% of World population	Source
World	6,920,300,000	24-May-11	100%	US Census Bureau's World Population Clock
Peoples Republic of China	1,399,724,852	1-Nov-10	19.36%	2010 China Census
India	1,210,193,422	1-Mar-11	17.49%	Provisional 2011 Indian Census result
United States	**311,411,000**	**24-May-11**	**4.50%**	**Official United States Population Clock**
Indonesia	237,556,363	10-May	3.43%	2010 Indonesian Census
Brazil	190,732,694	1-Aug-10	2.76%	2010 Official Brazilian Census results
Pakistan	176,129,000	24-May-11	2.55%	Official Pakistani Population clock
Nigeria	158,423,000	2010	2.29%	UN estimate for 2010
Bangladesh	150,608,000	24-May-11	2.18%	Official Bangladeshi Population Clock
Russia	142,905,200	1-Jan-11	2.07%	2010 Russian Census
Japan	127,960,000	1-Mar-11	1.84%	Official Japan Statistics Bureau
Mexico	112,336,538	15-Apr-11	1.62%	2010 final census result
Philippines	94,013,200	Mid-2010	1.36%	National Statistics Office medium projection
Vietnam	87,375,000	2011	1.26%	Official estimate
Germany	81,802,000	31-Dec-09	1.18%	Official estimate
Egypt	80,276,000	24-May-11	1.16%	Official Egyptian Population clock

Appendix F
World Population Rankings After Amendment Ratification

Country	Population	Date of estimate	% of World population	Source
World	6,920,300,000	24-May-11	100%	US Census Bureau's World Population Clock
Peoples Republic of China	1,399,724,852	1-Nov-10	19.36%	2010 China Census
India	1,210,193,422	1-Mar-11	17.49%	Provisional 2011 Indian Census result
Indonesia	237,556,363	10-May	3.43%	2010 Indonesian Census
Brazil	190,732,694	1-Aug-10	2.76%	2010 Official Brazilian Census results
Pakistan	176,129,000	24-May-11	2.55%	Official Pakistani Population clock
Blue Country	**163,161,751**	**(ratification)**	**2.36%**	**(pending ratification)**
Nigeria	158,423,000	2010	2.29%	UN estimate for 2010
Bangladesh	150,608,000	24-May-11	2.18%	Official Bangladeshi Population Clock
Red Country	**146,623,435**	**(ratification)**	**2.11%**	**(pending ratification)**
Russia	142,905,200	1-Jan-11	2.07%	2010 Russian Census
Japan	127,960,000	1-Mar-11	1.84%	Official Japan Statistics Bureau
Mexico	112,336,538	15-Apr-11	1.62%	2010 final census result
Philippines	94,013,200	Mid-2010	1.36%	National Statistics Office medium projection
Vietnam	87,375,000	2011	1.26%	Official estimate
Germany	81,802,000	31-Dec-09	1.18%	Official estimate
Egypt	80,276,000	24-May-11	1.16%	Official Egyptian Population clock

Appendix G
About the Author
Still living the American Dream

"Some are talkers, some are doers. I prefer to be the latter."
--Bob Jackson

I was raised on a small ten-acre farm in southern New Jersey. My family raised chickens and sold eggs door-to-door to eager customers in Woodbury, New Jersey. My father also worked at the Philadelphia Naval Shipyard for thirty years. The farm also produced strawberries, raspberries, sweet corn, and gooseberries. I was very involved with all of these operations from early childhood through high school, at which time I left the farm to attend college.
I have been a profitable entrepreneur since 1949

Pot Holders

In 1949, I made and sold over 1,000 pairs of jersey loop potholders for $0.15 each, or $0.25 a pair. All the income, less the cost of material, went into a savings account I planned to use for college expenses.

Garden Plowing

During the spring of my 6th, 7th, and 8th grade years, I furthered my entrepreneurial spirit by plowing gardens for many of homeowners in Clarksboro. I used the family Farmall Cub tractor, and I was paid whatever the homeowner offered. Invariably, they paid more than I would charge, which made me very happy.

Honey

I invested a portion of my earnings from plowing gardens into a bee hive in order to successfully raise bees for a Boy Scout merit badge. From 1953 to 1955, I started with one hive for my merit badge project. The second season, I bought five multiple "super" hives with more money made from plowing gardens. Premium honey was graded for lightness in color and was very competitively priced at about $0.30 a pint. I planted buckwheat (which the bees used help them produce darker honey), pointed the hives toward local wild flowers and nearby woods, and happily developed very dark honey. This dark honey was sold to my previous egg customers as genuine "pure" honey, not the commercial light honey found in the stores. I sold several thousand pints for about $1.25 a pint, and the demand still far exceeded the supply. Eventually, my mom developed an allergy to bee stings and the bee business had to be sold. The proceeds from selling my highly profitable bee hives were saved for college costs.

Environmental (Space) suits

From 1965-1967, during employment at United Nuclear Corporation in New Haven Connecticut, I was in charge of making naval nuclear fuel assemblies. One of the procedures required the operators to work in a pure argon atmosphere saturated with alcohol. United Nuclear could not buy any workable operator-protective suits anywhere. Full-body rocket fuel-handling protective suits failed from alcohol exposure. Even the designers of the space suits for NASA's Mercury and Gemini programs could not produce proper suits. So, I decided to use my engineering skills and design a suit. I designed and made workable suits in my basement that worked better than United Nuclear's expectations. I sold these suits to United Nuclear and expanded sales to Universal Cyclops in Pittsburgh who successfully used the suits for welding operators inside large argon filled assembly rooms. Consequently, Garrisue

Industries, Inc. was established to assist my expanding environmental suit business. I then bid on a large contract with Oak Ridge Laboratories for plutonium handling suits. I made the only workable sample that was required for the bid. However, the federal government did not want to risk a project with the key device being made in the basement of one person. The government gave my design to a large company to supply the product, and, of course, at a higher price. I also earned my Masters Degree and worked at Untied Nuclear for more than fifty hours a week during this time.

TRIAX

In 1974 I started TRIAX, a general metal fabrication business in distressed Benton Harbor, Michigan, during the recession of that same year. TRIAX was started with leased equipment and buildings from F.A. Long Company. Working capital for the business was from my savings from prior paychecks. No bank financing was available for my new business for two years. Starting a manufacturing business is tough. The business started with three full-time employees plus myself. TRIAX, Inc. expanded continuously through 1995, at which time there were about 100 families depending on TRIAX for employment and wages. TRIAX shipped throughout North America and did substantial export business.

In preparation for retirement, I sold off various sections of the company over a period of a couple of years in order to minimize the job loss rate the employees would face. The last part of the company was sold through bankruptcy in 1998; however, operations and employment were unaffected by the sale. During the twenty-four years of TRIAX including through the bankruptcy there was never a missed payroll, late or unpaid taxes, late bank payments, or any loss to any secured creditor.

Jackson International, Inc.

Jackson International, Inc. was established 1990, and continues to do business to this day. This company was sub chapter "S" incorporated in 1993. The primary purpose was to assist TRIAX and other companies with their international import and export business. Exports were to countries such as China, Brazil, Australia, Canada, Hungary and Mexico. Imports were primarily from China. The manufacturing of freight rail car parts was started in 2006 and is currently done in a 30,000 square-foot facility in Constantine, Michigan and a 24,000 square foot facility in Arkansas. Both facilities serve customers in the United States, Mexico, and Canada. My son John is a half owner and is president of the company. I am the CEO – age has its privileges.

I am a proven inventor and holder of the following patents:

6,807,774 – USA 10/26/04 - Greaseless Fulcrum for Railcar Door

6,659,018 – USA 12/9/03   - Dual Pawls for Railcar door operation

6,647,896 – USA 11/18/03 - Greaseless Railcar Door Hanger Assembly

6,397,978 – USA 1/4/02   - Railcar Handbrake

     782,502 – Australia 8/4/05

     201/7595 – South Africa 5/29/02

     ZL 01133069.4 - China 8/15/2007

6,273,219 – USA 8/14/01 - Railcar Pendulum Brake Beam

5,785,159 – USA 7/28/98 - Railcar Braking Mechanism

5,456,337 – USA 10/10/95 - Anti-Rotation Member for Railcar Brake Beam

     95/0263 – South Africa 2/28/98

     ZL94108719.0 – China 1/13/01

5,613,814 – USA 3/25/97   - Intermodal Shipping Securing Device

5,259,485 – USA 11/9/93   - Railcar Brake System

5,000,298 – USA 3/19/91 - Railcar Brake Beam

4,641,399 – USA 2/10/87 - Interconnecting Container Lock

3,678,727 – USA 7/25/72 - Tri-axially redrawn metal Tubing

    953,245 – Canada 8/20/74

    1,388,431 – Great Britain 7/23/75

    978,272 – Japan

    2,101,395 – France 3/31/72

I also have extensive employment working for other businesses:

Date:	Employer:	Occupation:
1955	Paulsboro Record, Paulsboro, NJ	Reporter for east Greenwich newspaper
1957	Del Monte canning house, Swedesboro, NJ	Quality control 12 hr days, 7 days a week normal Summer work
1958	Philadelphia Navy Yard	Student trainee, metallurgical assistant Summer work
1960	Alan Wood Steel Co., Philadelphia, PA	Steel producer (summer work) Assistant metallurgist – Major temper rolling process improvement
1961 – 1962	ACF Industries, Albuquerque, NM	Metallurgist = "Q" security clearance

		Redefined heat treatment for 6061 Al
		Developed titanium alloy welding
		Nuclear weapons mfg
1962 – 1963	Superior Tube Company	Senior Engineer - "L" security clearance
		Develpoed new processes for naval nuclear control rods
1964 – 1969	United Nuclear, New Haven, CT	Naval nuclear reactor mfg
		1964 Senior Engineer
		1965 Welding Superintendent
		1966 Production engineering Manager
		1968 Project manager
1969- 1970	Elwood Ivins Tube Co., Horsham, PA	P and L Plant Manager
		Steel and Stainless Tubing redraw Mill (Reference my tubing patent)
1971	Olin Corp, Alton, IL	Techincal Specialist - Army Ordinance and air bag manufacturer.
1972	Abbery Steel Co, Perth Amboy, NJ	Plant Manager – Steel fabricator.
1973 – 1974	Graver Tank, east Chicago IN	Project manager fro the construction of huge refinery tanks and

commerciall nuclear plant

construction needs

1974—   president and owner of

1998   TRIAX

The above history was for employment for wages. Since 1974 all of my income
has been from TRIAX and Jackson International as the owner and operator.
(See the Entrepreneur section). From 1998 to 2003, I was also the Chief
Engineer for YSD Industries, Youngstown, Ohio to facilitate the sale of TRIAX to
YSD Industries.

Family Status

I was born September 23, 1939 to Ora Mae and James L. Jackson in Woodbury,
New Jersey and was raised on a small farm in Clarksboro, New Jersey. I married
Barbara Ann Arndt on August 30th, 1975. Barbara is a graduate from Western
Michigan University with a Bachelor's Degree in Education and a Masters
Degree in Educational Leadership. She taught high school English in a rural
Michigan setting until 1978 when our first son, Scott, was born. From 1978 to
1998 she was a devoted homemaker. From 1998 to 2010, Barbara was a
certified English teacher at an at risk urban high school.

Our first son, Scott, is also a graduate of Western Michigan University with a
Bachelor's Degree in Education and a Master's Degree in Educational
Leadership. He is currently a certified high school English teacher.

John, our second-born son, is a graduate of Michigan State University with a
Bachelor's Degree in Mechanical Engineering and also holds an M.B.A. from

Michigan State University. He is currently the president of Jackson International, Inc. which is a manufacturer of railcar components.

As mentioned earlier, I was married prior to meeting Barbara. In 1960, I married Helen Sue Pfaffinger, who was the daughter of German immigrants. We had one son, Thomas. Helen and I decided to divorce in 1969 after nine years of marriage. Thomas has gone on to marry Judy Priest and has two daughters, Brandy and Theresa. Thomas is a graduate of Northwood University with a Bachelor's Degree in Business. Judy is a devoted homemaker, while Brandy and Theresa are currently pursuing college plans of their own. Like his father, Thomas is a proven innovator and family provider.

I have also been recognized for significant civic activities:

8/8/77 TRIAX Tube Co - Business Commendation – City of Benton Harbor City Council

1983 Bob Jackson – Citizen of the Year – Benton Harbor Kiwanis Club

1983 Bob Jackson – Engineer of the year – Blossom Land Chapter Michigan Society of Professional Engineers

10/17/83 Bob Jackson Commendation – City of Benton Harbor Commission

First business man to purchase a portion of a vacated foundry building

Prime recruiter of other businesses to buy Benton harbor Industrial property

Chairman of the Benton Harbor City Enterprise Zone (No Tax Zone)

5/23/84 Recognition for donation of a complete X-Ray unit to the Davis Memorial Hospital in Georgetown, Guyana. - Seventh-Day Adventists

6/11/87 1987 Twin Cities Area Small Business Person of the Year – Twin Cities Chamber of Commerce

6/11/87 Gold Award for 50% growth in 3 years - TRIAX Tube Co – Twin Cities Chamber of Commerce.

11/6/87 Expansion Award – TRIAX Tube Co – Twin Cities Area Chamber of Commerce

7/15/91 Special Tribute to TRIAX - Senate of the State Of Michigan

1991 U.S. Chamber of Commerce "Blue Chip" achievement award. One of 4 businesses recognized in Michigan

1992 Golden Stake Award to Bob Jackson – Cornerstone Alliance, Council of Commerce and Community Development

1993 Tigers Baseball Team Sponsor (1st Place) – Benton Harbor Little League

11/5/93 Certificate of award to TRIAX-DAVIS (owned by Bob Jackson) for job training – Berrien-Cass-Van Buren Private Industry Council.

1/24/94 1993 Platinum Stake Award to TRIAX Tube Co. for 100% Sales increase in 1993. – Cornerstone Alliance

1994 Fairplain Tigers Baseball Team Sponsor (1st Place) – Benton Harbor Little League

1995 Fairplain Baseball Team Sponsor (2nd Place) – Benton Harbor Little League

9/12/95 Certificate of Appreciation – The Air Brake Association.

9/15/97 Certificate of Appreciation – The Air Brake Association.

2006 Wabano District Chairman Service Award - Boy Scouts of America

I have an extensive community service record:

Member – 32 years - First Church of God of St Joseph
   Member - Missions Board - 2 years

Director – 10 years – Twin Cities Area Chamber of Commerce
   Chairman – Enterprise Zone (No Tax Zone) Committee
   Member – Legislative Committee

Director – 1 year – Cornerstone Alliance (Area Economic Development)

Delegate – 1 year – Governor's Conference on Small Business (Michigan)

Chairman – 10 years – City of Benton Harbor Enterprise Zone (No Tax Zone) Council

Director – 2 years – Benton Harbor Businessmen's Association

Member – 2 years – Benton Harbor City Venture Advisory Board

]Director – 10 years – CETA, JTPA and finally the Tri-County Private Industry Council (PIC)
  Federal Job Training and Placement Programs

Director – 2 years – Northwestern Berrien County Sanitary Land Fill Authority

Member – 50 years – American Society of Metals

Member – 45 years – National Society of Professional Engineers

Member – 25 years - Michigan Society of Professional Engineers

Member – 10 years – Rotary International – Paul Harris Fellow

Boy Scouts of America - Lifelong involvement
Executive Board Member – 4 years - Berrien County Republicans

100 Club Member, 4th Congressional District Committee, Precinct Delegate

Candidate for Michigan 4th Congressional District – 1982 and 1984

Federal Elections Committee registered and Reported

Withdrew before Republican primary vote

Benton Harbor, Michigan

Benton Harbor, a small city of about 12,000 citizens, became increasingly distressed from early 1960's through the 1980's. It became so distressed that during the late 1980's Benton Harbor was ranked as the most distressed city in the nation for three of those years. I was the leader for forming an Enterprise Zone for Benton Harbor. I implemented and chaired the Enterprise Zone from 1990 to 1993. During these few years there were 144 new and expanded businesses in Benton harbor hiring over 700 new private sector employees. City revenue increased fourfold. By 1993 Benton Harbor was transformed to one of the fastest expanding economies in the nation. The "Blue" and "Red" thinking people in and around Benton Harbor fought for the control of the Enterprise Zone and the ensuing "gridlock" stopped all job growth. Today, Benton Harbor is once again one of the most distressed cities in America.

Education:

east Greenwich Grammar School, Clarksboro, NJ - 1953

Swedesboro High School, Swedesboro, NJ - 1957

Government major scholarship (unfunded after competitive acceptance)

Track letter – 880 yard event and a school chinning record

Basketball manager letter

Several social clubs

Lehigh University, Bethlehem, PA 1961

    B.S. Metallurgical Engineering

    Dorm Social Chairman 2 years

    Married senior year

Rensselaer Polytechnic Institute 1968

    MS Industrial Management

Registered Professional Engineer (PA, IN)

I have a special commitment to the Boy Scouts of America:

6/1/51 through 5/31/54 – Registered with Troop 59, Clarksboro, NJ

    I was the Troop's first Eagle Scout with 33 merit badges and 2 palms

    I was the first in the troop to earn the God and Country award

1961 – Assistant Scoutmaster Albuquerque, NM

1963-64 – Scout Master, Collegeville, PA – Restarted an inactive troop

1986-87 - Cub Master, Hollywood, Stevensville, MI (Started this Pack)

2002 – 2006 – Wabano District Chairman, SW MI Council (4 years Quality District)

My Military Record is very limited

Registered 9/24/57 No. 28-20-39-451

Classified 2-S 11/5/57 (Student)

Classified 4-F 4/7/59 (Physical deferment after second Spinal fusion operation)

1957/58 One year (4 credits) ROTC – Lehigh University

Classified 3-A 8/6/63

Footnote

I had a spinal fusion during my senior year in high school and missed almost half a year in class. I was home-schooled for the almost four months of recuperation and made the honor roll for the same semester and year. During my freshman year of college the fusion broke and I had a second spinal fusion between my freshman and sophomore college years. In spite of these setbacks, I graduated as an engineer at the age of 21. The original "Get it done!"

www.ingramcontent.com/pod-product-compliance
Lightning Source LLC
Chambersburg PA
CBHW050130280326
41933CB00010B/1316